Shimla on Foot

TEN WALKS

Raaja Bhasin

RUPA

To
Dhruve and Raaghav,
troopers in the making.

Published by
Rupa Publications India Pvt. Ltd 2007
7/16, Ansari Road, Daryaganj
New Delhi 110002

Sales centres:
Allahabad Bengaluru Chennai
Hyderabad Jaipur Kathmandu
Kolkata Mumbai

ISBN: 978-81-291-1215-6

10 9 8 7 6 5 4 3 2

The moral right of the author has been asserted.

Typeset by Arrt Creations, New Delhi

Printed at Nutech Photolithographers, New Delhi

CONTENTS

Introduction

FOR THE YEARS WHEN SHIMLA WAS THE 'SUMMER CAPITAL' OF BRITISH India, only three horse-drawn carriages and later automobiles were allowed in town. These belonged to the viceroy, the commander-in-chief and the governor of the Punjab – the town's chief medical officer was the only exception and was allowed a car. The townspeople rode, used rickshaws or walked. The human pulled-and-pushed rickshaw is fortunately a thing of the past, the horses are there, but more for pleasure-rides than any serious movement. Inevitably, cars, buses and trucks are driven in today's Shimla – and yet, there is an interesting little distinction made among the 'older' and the 'newer' families in town. The 'old' ones all walk, the 'new' ones drive where they can. The old ones also attribute their health to the regular use of their legs. The privilege of living in Shimla, they say, is of being able to walk freely – not of driving over roads designed for pedestrians. Be this little distinction as it may, if you want to really see the town and experience the magic that is Shimla, you do have to walk.

While there is a level of physical effort involved, these walks are not exercise trails, but are designed to take you through the town's rich history, heritage and natural beauty. This is not a 'guide book' and there may be a few places of interest that are not on the walk routes in the book. However, the town's layout being largely pedestrian, most places have been covered here. At the same time and often enough, there will be alternative – and sometimes shorter – routes.

VII

The walks outlined here follow routes that have negligible or low vehicular traffic and touch places of interest. Shimla still has a somewhat complicated system of roads and for vehicles, these are divided into 'sealed', 'restricted' and 'open' ones. Most of the walks given here are along the sealed roads. While the Lower Bazaar is also taken as a short walk, most of the others attempt to skirt areas of dense population.

Some terms are used interchangeably, for example the former Viceregal Lodge now houses the Indian Institute of Advanced Study and both appear in the text. Time variations are there with every walk – and these depend on the pace you keep and the time taken for stopovers.

Himachal Tourism and the Shimla Municipal Corporation have placed plaques at various important sites around Shimla. The text of these has been prepared by the author and they may add a measure of interest to the walks.

Shimla — A Brief History

THE FINAL YEARS OF THE EIGHTEENTH CENTURY AND THE OPENING DECADES of the nineteenth, were a period of considerable turbulence in the hills of the Western Himalaya. The armies of Nepal had spilled over their borders and wrested control of large tracts of north India – including most of the present-day state of Himachal Pradesh. Deprived of their territories, many of the local hill chiefs approached the powerful East India Company for help. For a long time this assistance was not forthcoming and the normally peaceful tracts became a stage that displayed both rapacity and terror. Encouraged by their successes, this army of pillage began making inroads into areas that the British regarded as their own spheres of influence. The turning point came when the 'Gurkhas' – as these marauders had come to be called – began making damaging forays into the indigo plantations of today's Uttar Pradesh. This crop was vital for the 'Company Bahadur' as indigo was used to dye the uniforms of the Royal Navy.

Four armies were raised against the Gurkhas who were defeated in 1815. A formal end to the 'Gurkha Wars' came when the Treaty of Sagauli was signed the following year. The victorious British restored most of the hill kingdoms to their original rulers and decided to retain certain key positions as military outposts and as sanitaria.

One of these posts was Shimla, earlier spelt Simla. From a nondescript village whose name is variously reported as Shimlu,

Shemalaya, Semla, Shumla and Shemla, the town went on to become the 'summer capital' of British India. Another variation ascribes the origin of the place name to Shamla – blue, or dark lady – another name for the Hindu goddess Kali who is held in high veneration in these hills. In English, the spelling 'Simla' was used for most of the town's life while the start of the name had a gentler 'Sh' in the vernacular languages and was spelt 'Shimla'. In the 1980s, Shimla became the official spelling for the town.

The first house, built by a European in 1822, is regarded to be 'Kennedy House' which was the residence of Charles Pratt Kennedy, the newly appointed Political Officer to the Hill States. In 1827, the station was visited by Lord Amherst, the British Governor General of India, and the following year, the Commander-in-Chief, Lord Combermere also came to Shimla. The tract that holds the core of the town was acquired by the Governor General, Lord Bentinck in 1830 from the states of Patiala and Keonthal – who had earlier been given the lands for 'services rendered' during the Gurkha Wars.

In 1864, under the viceroyalty of John Lawrence, Shimla was officially declared the Summer Capital of the British Empire in India – a status it retained up to Indian Independence in 1947. Interestingly, the Government ended up spending more time in this little town than in the 'real' capitals, i.e. Kolkata (earlier, Calcutta) and later, New Delhi. The move to the hills usually took place in early April, and the migration back to the plains by late October or early November. And during this period, a staggering one-fifth of the human race was ruled from these heights, as the jurisdiction of the Indian Empire extended from Aden in the west to Myanmar (earlier, Burma) in the east. From 1871, the state government of the Punjab also began moving to Shimla from Lahore for the summer months.

X

Momentous political decisions that affect our lives to the present day were taken in Shimla – like some of the discussions that finally led to the independence and partition of India. In the post-independence era, the historic Simla Agreement was signed on 3 July 1972 between India and Pakistan. The Agreement declared that all issues between the two countries would be settled bi-laterally.

From 1947 to 1956, Shimla served as the state capital of the Punjab (then called 'East Punjab'). In 1966, the district of Shimla was transferred to the state of Himachal Pradesh. The town of Shimla and has since been its state capital.

Municipal governance was introduced as early as 1851; piped water was available from the 1880s; hydro-electric power was available by the early twentieth century; an engineering marvel of its time, the Kalka-Shimla railway line was completed in 1903; and one of the world's early 'automatic' telephone exchanges began functioning in Shimla by 1922.

As the summer capital, Shimla also saw a spate of remarkable building activity in town and some of the finest structures of the British-colonial genre still stand over its seven hills. Neo-Gothic vied with Tudor, and Norman baronial jostled for space with Swiss Bavarian chalets. Every possible construction medium used at the time found a place in Shimla. Stone could be as finely worked as the ashlar on the lower section of the Telegraph Office, the neat half-round dressing of the municipal offices or a raw stacking used to raise a cottage wall. Cast iron, brick, wood and mud (often mixed with pine needles), were used in various forms to create something akin to a fairyland. Window designs ranged from delicate sash, elaborate bay to complicated panes with diamond cuts. The range of columns on various structures ranged

XI

from Corinthian to Doric. In a word, architecture was eclectic and after the first shock, quite pleasing to the eye.

If Shimla's architecture formed a delightful potpourri, it was enhanced by its chocolate-box setting in the Lower Himalaya. Woods of oak and flowering rhododendron, pine and cedar surrounded the town. Ferns, mosses, lichens and wildflowers carpeted the slopes and this picture of idyllic retreat was framed by the snows of the northern peaks.

Today, the lingering strands of Shimla's past still echo through its streets and buildings, which are packed with history. In its old architecture, the town still holds the memory of Britain's imperial dream – made all the more fascinating because most of the designs are European while many structural elements are indigenous. The Mall with its resemblance to an English home county's marketplace has, perhaps, one of the longest stretches of pedestrian shopping anywhere in the world. The town also holds what may well be one of the last urban forests ever to be found on our planet.

The Seven Hills of Shimla

SOMEONE AT SOME POINT DECIDED THAT SHIMLA MUST BE AS IMPERIAL AS ancient Rome and found seven hills for the town. The seven hills keep changing their number and sometimes become eight and sometimes six. Be the number game as it may, the main hills that Shimla has are:

Prospect Hill – This is in western Shimla and has the temple of Kamna Devi. The initial part of the climb up the hill has some charming old houses that were a part of the former viceregal estate, the mid-section has some tasteless new ones and expectedly, the views from the top are quite amazing. Other parts of the hill are draped with oak woods.

Summer Hill – This, again, is in western Shimla. An early resident of Summer Hill, Colonel Mackenzie abandoned the area for the suburbs of Mashobra when he decided that the place had become too crowded. It then had three houses and now holds the entire campus of Himachal Pradesh University. The part of the university library that faces Shimla offers an excellent view. Past the campus, the woods still hold a good walk along the tarmac road.

Observatory Hill – This has the Indian Institute of Advanced Study, peripheral buildings, lawns, grounds and woods. The main building is housed in the magnificent former Viceregal Lodge. As the name suggests, this hill once held an observatory.

Inverarm (also called Mount Pleasant) – This too is in western Shimla. Its top houses the State Museum.

Bantony – Named after Governor General, Lord William Bentinck (1828-1835), this is in central Shimla. This rise holds the Grand Hotel.

Jakho – This is also in central Shimla and is the highest peak in the town. It is crowned by the temple of Bhagwan Hanuman.

The Elysium Spur – This is named after the 'Blessed Fields' of Greek mythology, a compliment given to Emily and Fanny, the sisters of Governor General, Lord Auckland (1835-1842). It extends from central Shimla to the northwest and holds the Auckland House School and Longwood. It extends up to the Bharari spur.

Most of the older sections of town are built around and over these hills. Of the newer sections, with substantial chunks of population, New Shimla lies below Bishop Cotton School and is built over what were open grasslands. And Sanjauli to the northeast extent of Jakho has grown considerably from a small village to hold hundreds of new structures.

WALK ONE

Where the White Man Carried his Burden

From Scandal Point to the former Viceregal Lodge.

DIRECTION, APPROXIMATE TIME AND DISTANCE

A round trip will cover approximately six kilometres along level stretches and slopes. Plan for around two hours – and depending on your interest and pace, this could well become a half-day walk.

From 'Scandal Point' on the Mall, this walk goes to the Indian Institute of Advanced Study, the former Viceregal Lodge and one of Shimla's 'must dos'. Zigzagging a little, the route is across the non-shopping areas of the Mall; and this walk is designed to include as many of the interesting sites that lie along or just off the track. Some places may seem to have been missed on the way while going, but are covered on the way back.

 SUGGESTED TIME OF THE DAY

You can choose to go for this walk at any time, except at night.

★ HIGHLIGHTS

Scandal Point
General Post Office (GPO)
St. Andrew's Church
Young Women's Christian Association
Bantony
Kali Bari Temple
Northbank (on a detour)
Railway Board Building
Gorton Castle
The Vidhan Sabha
Knockdrin
The Retreat, the Cecil and Cooper Block
State Museum
Armsdell
Viceregal Lodge (now, the Indian Institute of Advanced Study)
Yarrows
State Bank of India
St. Michael's Cathedral
Telegraph Office

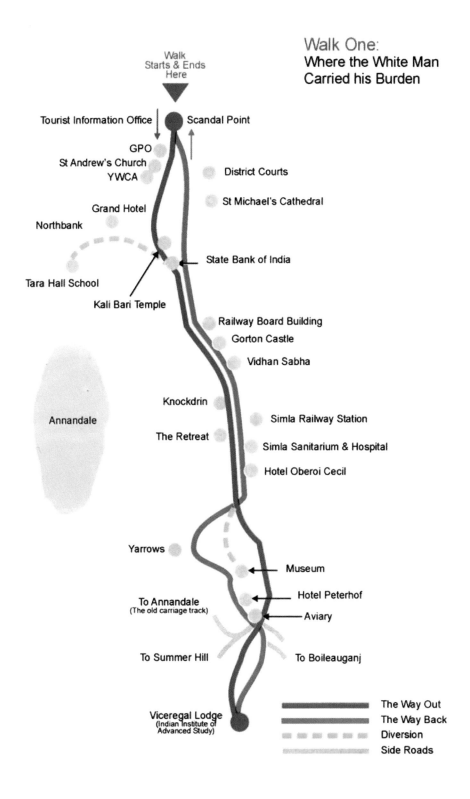

Walk One:
Where the White Man Carried his Burden

Walk Starts & Ends Here

Tourist Information Office
Scandal Point
GPO
St Andrew's Church
YWCA
District Courts
St Michael's Cathedral
Grand Hotel
Northbank
State Bank of India
Tara Hall School
Kali Bari Temple
Railway Board Building
Gorton Castle
Vidhan Sabha
Annandale
Knockdrin
Simla Railway Station
The Retreat
Simla Sanitarium & Hospital
Hotel Oberoi Cecil
Yarrows
Museum
To Annandale
(The old carriage track)
Hotel Peterhof
Aviary
To Summer Hill
To Boileauganj
Viceregal Lodge
(Indian Institute of Advanced Study)

The Way Out
The Way Back
Diversion
Side Roads

Scandal Point

'Scandal Point' is where the Mall, the route to the Ridge and that to the GPO meet. It is regarded by many to have got its name from the unfounded tale that it was the place from where an erstwhile Maharaja of Patiala carried off a British commander-in-chief's daughter. While Bhupinder Singh, the Maharaja in question, is known to have cut a figure that was more than dashing, it is unlikely that he or the lady (whom he is supposed to have swung over his saddle), would have been out on the streets airing their love. What is more likely is that this central position of the town's fashionable promenade, the Mall, has for long seen people gathering to both converse and gossip and these two were predictably drawn into the excitement. Here governments have risen and fallen, borders have collapsed or sprung up; here the world has changed in a span of seconds, and here salacious whispers have been exchanged, not only about who ran off with whom, but also about who would like to run off and with whom.

The first leg of this walk goes past the ICICI Bank (which used to be Grindlay's Bank), to touch the half-timbered structure of the General Post Office. The intervening stretch has held banks, commercial establishments and offices through most of Shimla's past. Till their recent reconstruction, this stretch had ornate wooden buildings in the Swiss Bavarian style of architecture characterised by exposed woodwork that was elaborately turned, fret-worked and corbelled. One early twentieth century writer likened this stretch of establishments to 'an elaborate mantelpiece'.

3

General Post Office

The half-timbered building of the GPO was completed on 3 July 1883. This was originally a house named Conny Lodge, which was purchased from its owner, Mr Peterson – the proprietor of the town's first firm of European tailors, Messrs Enjalberg and Co. Peterson later became Manager of the Simla Bank. An interesting element of its design lay in the six large hollow pillars of stone and brick that traversed its height. Up to 1920, firewood was lit inside these pillars to warm the building.

Till the coming of the railway in 1903, mail used to reach Shimla on horse-drawn *tongas*. Then, special red-painted 'mail rickshaws' pulled and pushed by four men would deliver the mail bags from the railway station to the GPO and to the sub-post offices. Overseas mail, the *valaiti dâk*, often arrived at night and was delivered immediately. A red flag was hoisted on the building's tower to announce its arrival while a *chaprassi*, office messenger, carrying a hand bell would summon the postmen from the adjoining residential quarters to deliver it. A fire in the 1970s damaged the building heavily and it was then rebuilt, retaining the essentials of the original design, that had once been passed off as 'wild west gothic' by a diligent observer.

The Mall below

Conventionally lined by buildings and trees, a 'Mall' was a promenade free of traffic and if it held commercial establishments, then shopping added its own colour to the social aspect of things.

At one point of time, Shimla's Mall was regarded to be as fashionable as the finest streets of London, Paris or St. Petersburg and every morning, the tarmac was washed down by *mashkis* –

so called after the 'mashk', a goatskin bag filled with water that they had strapped to their backs. Once a major determinant of the town's character and social ethos, today the Mall stands largely divested of its colonial and rather snooty ambience. Yet, the original architecture still forms its spine and the street remains the town's social hub, albeit shorn of the more blatant social divisions it once witnessed. For many, the Mall is also an economic axis. There is hardly a person who lives in Shimla who regards his day as complete without a daily salute to its tarmac or an evening promenade. There is hardly a visitor who will not rush there on his very first day in town. Motor vehicles are still not allowed through its core. Only select cars that carry dignitaries, and ambulances and fire engines may ply through the street. Barring the latter two emergency services, the others are not really welcome and it is noteworthy that in this age of howling sirens and gun-toting jeeps, even incumbent ministers have stepped out of their cars to walk along this stretch.

5

Do take a moment to look down at the Mall from this point. The roofline changes with every structure and decorative elements like the skylights and columns also change. An interesting example of window design can be seen on the upper floor of the Indian Coffee House, where bay windows have been given a lotus shape. Given the cheek by jowl character of the buildings along the street, safety and fire prevention came into play with the 'fire walls'. The buildings have their walls rising a couple of feet over the roofs to contain flames and prevent fires from spilling over into the adjoining structures. The efficacy of these has been amply demonstrated several times.

One example is the fire that had gutted the – now rebuilt – Jankidas Building, which held the famous restaurant Davico's, while its neighbours escaped relatively unscathed. Named after the brothers who initially ran it, this restaurant used to be a Shimla landmark. It was renowned for its huge hall that was held up without the support of pillars.

Retaining Walls

This is also a point to delve into what may seem a rather silly thing to be found staring at – the retaining walls. Practically all of Shimla's old revetments are built of dressed stone that has been set without the use of mortar and the wear of passing decades has shown their efficiency. So, while the new retaining walls have collapsed at the first sight of rain, these old ones have shrugged, settled a little, at best twirled a lichen or two, and simply stayed on. Covered with a variety of mosses and wildflowers, especially the delicate daisy-like summer starwort, the botanical *erigeron*, they add considerable character to the town.

St. Andrew's Church

The hill immediately behind the Post Office holds the deconsecrated church of St. Andrew's, the Church of Scotland. The site first belonged to the Union Church that was built by W.H. Carey in 1869. In 1905, it was gazetted as the Scots Kirk of Shimla, and on 30 August 1914 the Viceroy, Lord Harding set the memorial stone that read,

'This Kirk was
Biggit Be Godlie
Men in the year
Of our Lord 1914.'

Completed in May 1915, the structure was named St. Andrew's Church and its decorative cornerstones are the only concession to its Spartan brick façade. The building now houses a wing of the State Library and is a treasure trove of rare books. Adjoining this is the Manse, now the Evening College, and the site of the oldest houses in Shimla.

The Young Women's Christian Association (YWCA)

By the Manse and above the road, is the YWCA in a wooden structure called Constantia, and is on the site of one of Shimla's earliest houses – that even vied for the position of being the first. In the early twentieth century, the property was owned by the Delhi and London Bank from whom it was purchased by the Government for housing the Meteorological Department. In 1907, it was decided by the governor general in council to establish the YWCA at this location. So, work began on rebuilding the house in what is locally called the *dhajji* style of construction, which uses

7

lath and plaster. This was opened for residence on 22 October 1910 by Lady Minto who accompanied her husband, Viceroy of India, Earl Minto.

Dhajji **and praise of Lath and Plaster**

Most of Shimla's old houses employed a standard timber-framed structure – *dhajji*. These lath and plaster houses were conditioned to a European floor plan and the load-bearing wooden posts were set into shallow but stable foundations. The vertical members were then spanned by horizontal beams creating a wooden mesh. Within each square, normally about two feet by two, corner to corner wooden planks were fitted in a diagonal cross. The open space was filled in with stone held together by a mortar of clay, slaked lime and in later years, even cement. In some, baked brick was used for the infill. This was then plastered over, completely on the inside and at times, only partially on the exterior, leaving the main wooden frame decoratively exposed in the Tudor fashion. Variations were made by adding pine needles or straw into the mortar, and this provided greater binding power as well as insulation.

Practical and once inexpensive, the building style also had a considerable seismic response due to its inherent elasticity. When the town was hit by an earthquake in 1905, it came away practically unscathed, while nearby Kangra was as good as ruined and at least a portion of the blame was placed on its stone structures.

Bantony

On your left, you will see the upper sections of the Telegraph Office. A few yards ahead, and you are at the former Police Headquarters in a building named Bantony. This has some delightfully eccentric woodwork with corbelling and turning and a foliated pagoda over the porch. This was the residence of the erstwhile rulers of the princely state of Sirmaur; and the remnants of the cast-iron railings still display their coat of arms. Perhaps even more interesting and in a similar architectural vein, is the tumbledown cottage by the side, which was an annexe to the main house and now houses the Employment Exchange. The cabbage palms that still grow by the gate are one of the few of this plant species that can withstand Shimla's winter temperatures. The rise ahead holds the Grand Hotel, which was once Lord William Bentinck's residence.

The Grand Hotel

In 1829, the Grand Hotel was the site of a *dâk* bungalow, an accommodation for travellers. This was dismantled and rebuilt to provide the first residence for a governor general. It was named Bentinck Castle after its first occupant, Lord William Bentinck. In

1830, Lord Bentinck negotiated and acquired the land from the rulers of Patiala and Keonthal to form the core of Shimla.

Subsequently, the house became the residence of various British commanders-in-chief of the Indian Army – Sir Henry Fane, Sir Jasper Nicholls and Sir Hugh Gough. It then became the property of the famous Sir Henry Lawrence, brother of the Viceroy, Sir John Lawrence. The Simla Bank became its next owner and this was the site of the fortifications erected by the British residents of Shimla to ward off any attack during the Great Uprising of 1857. In time, and with ornate woodwork, this became the famous Peliti's Grand Hotel built by the celebrated confectioner and amateur photographer, the Chevalier Peliti. The original building, built almost entirely of wood, was destroyed by a fire in 1922. The rebuilt structure now serves as the Central Government Employees' Holiday Home and still carries the name of its former glory.

The view from this stretch of road is of the southern valley of Shimla, which is the site of the temple of Dhanu Devta, and is outlined in the walk titled 'Down Southern Slopes'. The hill across is called Tara Devi named after the goddess whose temple is located at its top. In the evening, you can see the lights of Kasauli and Subathu; and on an exceptionally clear evening, just after a bout of rain you may just be able to glimpse the river Satluj as it flows through the plains of the Punjab.

Kali Bari Temple

Past the Grand Hotel is the temple of Kali Bari. This was founded in 1845 by Ram Charan Bhramachari, a Bengali Brahmin. The temple, one of the oldest in Shimla, is held in high veneration by the town's Hindu community and is dedicated to the Goddess

Kali. While a black marble image occupies the central position in the sanctum, it is flanked by vermillion daubed stone carvings which are considered to be the images that were unearthed from the site of the 'original' temple. The apocryphal story is that the original temple with these images lay on the slopes of Jakho, near what is now Rothney Castle. The temple was demolished by a European settler and the images flung down the hill. The goddess visited him in a dream and the contrite man had the present temple initiated. The Kali Bari temple is open to all, but shoes must be removed outside and there are some restrictions on photography. A side shrine dedicated to Bhagwan Shiva was built in the late twentieth century.

A *Detour to* Tara Hall

Just past the temple gates a sharp flight of stairs leads down to Fingask, the Catholic Club, Northbank and the convent at Tara Hall.

At the foot of the stairs a short level road turns right to Fingask Estate. The birthplace of a former Viceroy of India, Lord Chelmsford, this was once the Chelmsford Club. The old house has been girdled by new concrete structures and narrow alleys. Adjoining this is the former Catholic Club in Ensham Estate's old building, and for many years this served as the residence of the German consul general. Neither functions as a club today – but despite years of neglect, the latter still has some interesting architecture. Continue down past the gates of the Catholic Club, on the road that leads to Kaithu. Less than a hundred yards down, there is bench on the road. On its right a level path goes past a branch of the ECI (Evangelical Church of India) Chalet Day School to a largely forgotten landmark of town, Northbank – the

11

one-time residence of celebrated author, Rudyard Kipling.

Returning to the plunging slope, past the Pineview Hotel and the Mythe (once the residence of the Maharaja of Dumraon), is the Convent at Tara Hall. In 1870, Tara Hall belonged to Major S.B. Goad, one of Shimla's largest house owners. This was then purchased by the Government; and once accommodation was created in the vicinity of the former Viceregal Lodge, this was resold to Colonel J. Robertson who had served as President of the Simla Municipality. It then provided the site for a Convent that was established in 1895, by the Loreto Order of Ireland with accommodation for a hundred boarders and three hundred day pupils. The buildings were rebuilt in 1930 with functional brick and concrete. An adjoining property, called Wheatfield – and later, Darbanga House, when it passed into the hands of the Maharaja of Darbanga – was also purchased by the Convent in the 1960s and integrated with the school.

From here, backtrack up the slope. At its head and by the stairs leading up to Kali Bari, turn right along the level road to the State Bank of India and rejoin the primary walk route.

St. Mark's and Prakash Bhavan

After the temple gates, the primary walk takes a sharp slope that turns left and tests the strength of your knees. Halfway down is the deconsecrated structure of St. Mark's. In 1875, St. Mark's served as the Home Office and then, as the YMCA. The Union Church also occupied a portion of the building. An excellent example of site utilisation, the structure employs a combination of *dhajji*, lath and plaster, dressed stone and brick while moving up the hill in steps. Air vents that allowed the space under the floorboards to breathe freely can clearly be seen along the walls of this building. In modern architecture, this style with overlapping roofs, is similar to the one made popular by Frank Lloyd-Wright.

Our walk route loops behind the State Bank of India to rejoin the Mall at Prakash Bhavan that houses the Simla Typewriter Company. Prakash Bhavan was earlier called Berodel, when its owner, Mr Banker named it after his daughters. It is an interesting example of varied materials used in construction – the lowest level has dressed stone, followed by brick and topped by *dhajji*.

The Railway Board Building

Built in 1896-97, this unusual cast-iron and steel structure once held the offices of the Railway Board and the Department of Commerce. Constructed at a time when safety was a core consideration for official buildings throughout the British Empire, this was designed to be structurally fire-resistant – and a recent blaze has testified to this. In Shimla, the present-day secretariat of the government of Himachal Pradesh at Ellerslie, and the offices of the Army Training Command (the former offices of the commander-in-chief of the Indian Army) also employed this building technique to a substantial extent.

The building was originally designated as the Public Works Department Secretariat offices and was fabricated by the Bombay based firm, Richardson and Cruddas. Above road level, the building has four levels and with one side exposed, climbing down the hill, it has three 'basements'. Most of the material – including the huge girders – was transported to Shimla in bullock carts and then riveted and bolted into position.

This still houses various government offices and retains all its unusual majesty.

Gorton Castle and the Himalaya Brahmo Samaj

On the wooded rise ahead is the present-day office of the accountant general of Himachal Pradesh in Gorton Castle, one of the most striking examples of British colonial architecture. In the nineteenth century there was a house here called Gorton Castle that belonged to a Mr Gorton of the Indian Civil Service. From Mr Gorton, the house changed hands a few times till this was purchased by Sir James Walker, of the Alliance Bank of Simla and a prominent resident of the town. He donated the site to the townspeople for the construction of a hospital for Europeans and Eurasians. Even then, the location was considered inappropriate for a hospital and with the consent of Sir James, another site was adopted for the hospital. Meanwhile, this piece of land was

purchased by the Government of India, for the construction of its secretariat.

With a floor area of around 12,500 metres, this neo-Gothic structure was designed by the famous architect, Sir Samuel Swinton Jacob. Jacob was an engineer, architect and writer who entered the Bombay Artillery in 1858, qualifying five years later as a surveyor

14

and engineer. After initial service in the Public Works Department, and a brief spell with the Aden Field Force, he was appointed as Executive Engineer to the former princely state of Jaipur – where he spent his entire working life. And it is from his experience and admiration of Indian architecture that we find the unique element of the Rajasthani *jaali* work on its balconies.

Jacob's design was modified during the course of construction and the work was superintended by Major H.F. Chesney of the Royal Engineers. The stone for the building came from the quarries near Sanjauli and after dressing, this was set in lime.

Completed in 1904, this was the secretariat of the Imperial Government of India and housed the Legislative, Finance, Lands, Education and Health departments.

Facing the gates of the building, the fork on the left leads to the railway station and the walk route takes the road to the right. On the northern path and walking in Gorton Castle's shadow, the snow peaks of the Greater Himalaya are visible and the large grey structure with bright red roofs in the foreground is the Convent at Tara Hall. Immediately ahead, and below the road is the temple of the Himalaya Brahmo Samaj built in 1886; the Samaj, or society was a Hindu reform movement which was started early in the nineteenth century by Raja Ram Mohun Roy in Bengal. This was never very active, but maintained a quiet presence in Shimla.

The Vidhan Sabha and just after

On the left, just after Gorton Castle lie the chambers of the Vidhan Sabha of Himachal Pradesh; this is the Assembly of Legislators. In the days before the Independence of India in 1947, this imposing structure served as the Legislative Assembly

Chamber of India. Built of white stone and brick, this was designed by a Mr W. George of Delhi and was completed in 1921. The creation of this building was a direct result of the Montagu-Chelmsford (Montford) constitutional reforms announced in 1919, when larger premises were required to house the expanded Legislative Assembly.

The same rise once held Kennedy House. This was built in 1822 and is regarded to have been the first 'permanent' house built by a European in Shimla. Today, no trace of the structure is visible and now the site serves as the parking lot of the Vidhan Sabha. Below the road, on the right, is Race View that despite its dilapidated condition is a good example of how the difficult terrain was effectively utilised and how access was given at different levels. In all likelihood, Race View got its name from the races that were then held at Annandale, and is a typical old Shimla house built of lath and plaster. In the 1920s this held the establishments of the superintending engineers, Shimla East and West Divisions.

A fork on the right, by the Army Mess at Knockdrin, leads to the Glen and to Annandale. These are outlined as separate walks. Knockdrin was once the residence of the foreign secretary. In the British Isles, Knockdrin and its castle are in Ireland, north of Mulligar and the name of this large double-storeyed bungalow may well have come from there. One resident of Shimla's Knockdrin was Sir Mortimer Durand, after whom the famous football tournament is named – which was initially played at Annandale.

On the left, in a *dhajji* and brick house called Kennedy Cottage, are the offices of the Central Public Works Department. It was in 1885 that the Simla Imperial Circle of the C.P.W.D. came into being, with Henry Irwin as its Superintending Engineer. Irwin was the architect of some of Shimla's important buildings like the Viceregal Lodge, the old Town Hall (that housed the Gaiety Theatre) and of Ripon Hospital.

This is as good a moment as any to take a look at the cast-iron bases of Shimla's old street lamps. George V was King when Shimla got its electricity in 1913 and his coat of arms was placed here. The emblems were unscrewed into storage after Independence and the blank space on each of the lamps marks their absence.

Cleremont

The large bland office building on the left is Cleremont that was built in 1927-28 in a combination of *dhajji* and of stone set in mud. The original purpose of this structure was to house the offices of the inspector general, Imperial Service Troops and the inspector general of explosives in India. Later, it housed the offices of the director, Frontier Circle and the director general of the Survey of India. At various times this building has also held the offices of the Central Board of Revenue, the director general of Posts and Telegraphs, the Ex-Services Association, India and the Department of Industries and Labour.

Cleremont is followed by Woodbank, a *dhajji* and wood house that belongs to the Railways.

The Retreat, the Sanitarium and the Cecil

Past this, on the right, is the Retreat, the residence of the army commander. This was built in 1905 as the residence for individual members of the viceroy's executive council. Till it swung back to its original name, it was simply called Command House for several

17

years – after General Thimmaya, G.O.C. in C. of the Western Command (25 March 1954 to 14 May 1955) occupied it and found the name inappropriate for a soldier. The wood and *dhajji* façade of the structure remains largely unchanged to the present-day. A variation in the roof of the Retreat was made by using Febro Cement tiles in place of the standard corrugated iron sheets.

After the Retreat, is the sanitarium run by the Seventh Day Adventists. This was originally a guest house named Carton House built of brick and *dhajji*, till Dr H.C. Menkel shifted the sanitarium and chapel to this position from Belvedere in the Lakkar Bazaar area, during the 1940s. Dr Menkel had basically created a hydro and spa here, till Dr I.R. Bazliel took over in 1949 and modified the premises to serve as a hospital.

This is followed by the exhaustively restored hotel, the Cecil. The Cecil Annexe that lies on your right with its rough-cast walls still displays the original architecture of the buildings. At the site of the Cecil stood a house called the Tendrils, which was occupied by the celebrated writer Rudyard Kipling for a season in the 1880s. And it was from the Cecil that the hotelier M.S. Oberoi started his legendary career when he joined the establishment as a humble desk clerk.

After the hotel, again on the left, is the Cecil's Cooper Block that despite its somewhat weathered look has some remarkable architectural forms – especially in the decorative windows and their alpine look.

Rudyard Kipling

The writings of Rudyard Kipling have been enjoyed for well over a century and a quarter, and India played a major role in the texture and character of his work. The son of Alice and Lockwood Kipling, Rudyard was born in Bombay (now Mumbai) in 1865. At the age of six he and his sister Trix were sent to England to be educated. Still in his teens, he returned to India and took a job as a journalist with Lahore's *Civil and Military Gazette*. He finally left India at the age of twenty-three.

Awarded the Nobel Prize for Literature in 1907, his 'India writings' include *Kim, The Jungle Books, Plain Tales From The Hills* and *Wee Willie Winkie* – which has that remarkable story 'The Man Who Would Be King'. The British Empire, army life, the sea, and men and machines have all played a part in the works of the man who has been called a 'romantic working within a stoic framework'.

Parts of India and his numerous acquaintances have found their cameo roles in his writings. And some important settings are in Shimla and Lahore. A tour in 1887 of Rajasthan's princely states, created a series of articles and that story of intrigue, *The Naulakha*; the fabulous ruins he saw entered the *Jungle Book* as Mowgli's 'Cold Lairs' with its monkeys and snakes. With inimitable evocations of the country and its people, Kipling once said of India, that it must be 'one's whole life or nothing'.

Rudyard Kipling spent his last years in the Sussex countryside where he died in 1936.

Shimla, on which he wrote some more fables, is found wheeling over the pages of *Plain Tales from the Hills*, and in the story where a "phantom 'rickshaw" stalks Jack Pansay. Then there are certain poems and of course, *Kim*. In the latter, Lurgan Sahib was based on a real-life Shimla character – the dealer of gemstones, A.M. Jacob after whom the famous Jacob diamond is named.

The State Museum

Open from 10 a.m. to 5 p.m. on all days except Mondays and gazetted holidays. There is no entry charge.

A sharp climb of half a kilometre takes you to the State Museum at Inverarm atop Mount Pleasant. A trip to the museum may be included in this walk or taken separately. The museum has a display of Himachal's heritage but unfortunately, it has nothing on Shimla. In the last quarter of the nineteenth century, the house was totally rebuilt of stone set in mud and was often allotted to members of the viceroy's council. In the 1860s this belonged to General Innes, who also owned several other properties in Shimla. This then became the property of the Raja of Sirmaur and was later purchased by the Government. Its occupants included Lord William Beresford who contributed greatly to the civic development of Shimla, General Sir Edwin Collen, Sir Edward Law, Sir Sankaran Nair, Sir Mohamed Shafi and Sir Mohamed Habibullah.

There is a short-cut from the museum that leads to the Hotel Peterhof and on to the little aviary. And like all self-respecting shortcuts, this is an unpaved, somewhat rocky path with designs on unwary ankles. If you decide to take this, just after the aviary you will find yourself at the gates of the Indian Institute of Advanced Study. Backtracking is however suggested down the slope. The base of the climb to the museum has two roads – like arms – that encircle the hill. Both take you to the gates of the Institute. If you face them, with your back towards the Cecil, then the fork on the right is the route taken, while the return is along the other road.

Towards the Radio Station

A couple of minutes along a road shaded by trees of Himalayan oak, you will find four concrete rockets lashed together and grounded against their will. This is the Radio Station and the site once held the Foreign Office in a house called The Valentines. During the Second World War, the Government of Burma (now, Myanmar) in Exile was based here. When the state of Himachal Pradesh came into being its secretariat was located here and the building was renamed Himachal Dham. This burned down and was replaced by this windowless wonder.

Above is the modern construction of the Hotel Peterhof. Up to the time of the construction of Viceregal Lodge atop Observatory Hill, this site served as the viceroy's residence in Shimla and the large *dhajji* bungalow was called Peterhof: so named as 'Doz', the anonymous writer of *Simla in Ragtime* (1913) quipped, with the express purpose of making the Russians feel at home when they came visiting. Before moving off, one viceroy called it a 'shooting box', while another declared it to be nothing

21

but a pigsty. This became another one of Shimla's fire-casualties. Interestingly, as with many other sites in Shimla, this is a natural watershed where the wash from the southern slope flows down towards the Bay of Bengal, and from the northern slope, towards the Arabian Sea.

Armsdell

On the right lies Armsdell, the present-day residence of the chief justice of Himachal Pradesh. This was originally built as a single-storey house in 1888. A double-storeyed kitchen, the servants' quarters, stables and a rickshaw shed were added as outhouses. A tennis court was also created here in 1907-08. As a part of the former viceregal estate, this was rebuilt in 1939-40 of brick set in cement mortar with rough-cast walls. The roofing was done with galvanised iron sheeting in the Nainital pattern. With elements of the art deco style of architecture, the house still retains its original character.

Rain and monkeys on tin roofs

What were called 'tin roofs' were actually made of galvanised iron that had begun to arrive in Shimla soon after their mass production began in Britain in the 1840s. In no time at all, this became the standard norm of roofing in town and in practically every other 'hill station' across the country. The corrugated sheet was more commonly used than the flat sheet. The latter, with ridges over wooden battens was termed the Nainital pattern – after that other hill station in the present-day state of Uttaranchal – and was used for the extra stylisation of houses.

Most of the early European houses in Shimla had roofs of beaten earth where the occupants sometimes had to move around indoors with open umbrellas. Locally quarried slate or slabs of quartzite, shingles (including wooden ones) and tiles that were used for roofing, were increasingly replaced by this medium. The steady drumming of rain on these roofs has almost become an iconic image of an Indian hill station, while the din and clash of monkeys on them can disconcert any new visitor.

The Burj and others

There are a couple of attractive old houses along this stretch; on the right, The Burj with its slate cladding on a wall, neat gables and tall chimney stacks, has a well preserved façade. This was built in 1876 to receive the Indian princes when they called on the viceroy at Peterhof; later this was the residence of the viceregal surgeon.

A short sharp slope also climbs to the little aviary and can easily be included in this walk. This aviary is home to common pheasants and other birds.

Passing a small open space on the road, we are now at the gates of the Indian Institute of Advanced Study. This is also the point from where some other walks begin:

a.   The *Potters' Hill Walk*. This is to the right of the gates.

b.   The *Prospect Hill Walk*. This is to the left.

c.   The old carriage track to Annandale – mentioned towards the end of the *Annandale Walk*. This goes down to the right, just after the teashop by the gates.

23

The Indian Institute of Advanced Study (the former Viceregal Lodge)

Open from 9 a.m. to 6 p.m. Visitors are allowed in the lawns and a portion of the interior in groups accompanied by a guide. Ticket for entry costs Rs 25 for Indians and Rs 50 for foreigners. The Institute remains closed if a seminar is on.

As the site for the viceroy's palace, this position atop Observatory Hill was selected by Lord Lytton, Viceroy of India between 1876 and 1880. The plans were shelved by his successor Lord Ripon who was happy enough with Peterhof and wryly remarked, 'I think it will last my time.' In Lord Dufferin's tenure (1884-88), the plans were redrawn and the Lodge built. He occupied what Doz called 'a joy and an expense forever', for the last few months of his stay in India. While the overall plan was suggested by Dufferin himself, Henry Irwin was the architect and F.B. Hebbert and L.M. St. Clair were associated as executive engineers.

The building resembles a Scottish baronial castle and is built of light blue-grey stone masonry with tiled pitch roofing. Most of the stone was quarried at the foothills town of Kalka and transported here in convoys of bullock carts. The main block has three storeys and the kitchen wing has five. A tower strikes above the rest of the structure and its height was increased during the viceroyalty of Lord Curzon (1899-1905). In Lord Irwin's time, a public entry wing was added in 1927. Major additions to the lawns were made by Lord Curzon and Lord Minto (1905-10). The interior has

remarkable woodwork of Burma teak; and this was the first building with electric lighting in Shimla.

Crucial discussions relevant to the independence and the partition of India were held in this very building. After Independence in 1947, the building became the property of the President of India and was renamed Rashtrapati Niwas. In 1964, the Indian Institute of Advanced Study was housed here at the behest of the then President, Dr S. Radhakrishnan.

The elaborate gateway of the Lodge was called the Gurkha Gate as it was manned by these legendary soldiers. The driveway up to the Institute's building is lined with oak and rhododendron trees. There is a smattering of deodar (Himalayan cedar), pine, spruce and a couple of Himalayan yews as well.

Within the estate, stroll towards the back and the terraces left by Lord Minto (Viceroy, 1905-10), where his coat of arms is still on display. These are connected by steps with stone balustrades. Somewhat worse for wear, a sundial and a map of the peaks and other landmarks visible from the spot are also here. Turn back for the glasshouse, above which is a rose pergola designed by Lord Curzon.

If you would like to spend some time in the woods around Viceregal Lodge, veer back along the way you came up. Walk down about a hundred metres where there is a bench and a narrow level road on the valley side. This leads to Squire's Hall, now the residence of the Institute's director. The narrow road passes through woods of oak and rhododendron and finally arrives at the university campus at Summer Hill. (This path's connection with the university campus is a tenuous one, as sometimes the gates are shut.) This walk is planned with a turn-around at Squire's Hall or a return from the Lodge.

Should you wish to know more about Viceregal Lodge, a small booklet is sold at the ticket booth. Guides are present to take you through the portion of the building which is open to visitors. There is a small cafeteria on the grounds which includes an outdoor sit-out and offers a pleasant view of the valley and the hills across.

If you have decided against a dip down to Squire's Hall, then leave the Institute's main building and head back. With the fire station of the Institute before you, avoid the route you took climbing up and take the fork on your right. This also leads to the Gurkha Gate and allows for a varied view en route. Behind the fire station and within the same structure, is an indoor

swimming pool, now in disuse. The rise immediately behind the pool has the Institute's guest house that was once the residence of the viceroy's private secretary.

On this route and still loosely tethered to the old viceregal estate is what was once the All Saints' Chapel – for which it would seem, with its little wooden spire and red shingle roof, the word 'charming' was invented. Now just holding on by the architectural equivalent of the 'skin of its teeth', this lies just after the bollards and chain on the way down by this side road. The access is by a short narrow path that lies by the large metal water tanks.

The way back

At the level space by the gates, with your back towards them, take the road on the left that lies before the holiday home called

Vishram and extends up to Ava Lodge. The former is a low neo-Tudor framed building that belongs to the Ministry of Health and Family Welfare.

This road will bring you to the base of the climb to the museum, close to the Cecil. On this track, the views of the hills to the north are quite magnificent and you will see a wide spread of the snow clad peaks; and if it is early spring, the rhododendrons will be in bloom. Wild raspberries and strawberries may also be sighted here; and in the monsoons, this is packed with tree ferns and a variety of other vegetation. Along the way, you skirt Ava Lodge on the hillside above. Ava Lodge was once the official residence for members of the viceroy's council and now serves as a hostel.

Below, on the left, lies Yarrows, designed by Sir Herbert Baker who built several structures in South Africa and was associated with Sir Edwin Lutyens in the creation of New Delhi. Yarrows, for a period, housed individual members of the council. Its large slate roof now holds a wing of the Indian Academy of Audit and Accounts; and briefly, the founder of Pakistan, Mohammed Ali Jinnah too lived here. Along the road, as part of the Academy complex, are two new buildings named Willows and Aster. And further up, all packed up in corrugated sheets, is a house called Holcombe.

From this point on, up to the State Bank of India, the walk backtracks along the earlier route.

The State Bank of India and ahead

At the State Bank, follow the Mall by taking the wider road on the right. The neo-Tudor structure of the bank is marked with exposed woodwork and pebbledash walls and it was constructed

28

in the early twentieth century. It originally housed the Bank of Bengal and later, the Imperial Bank of India.

Past the bank, on your right, lie the headquarters of the Army Training Command (ARTRAC). These large buildings which were described by one writer as 'a cross between a Balmoral and a jail', once held the headquarters of the Western Command. And before Independence, the headquarters of the commander-in-chief of the Indian Army were located here.

St. Michael's Cathedral

Again on the right, after the army offices, is the Catholic Church, St. Michael's Cathedral. Leave the main road to explore this superb dressed stone structure. When Lord Ripon came to India as Viceroy in 1880, this site was selected by him for the church of the town's Catholic community. Completed in 1886, this is built with a partial vocabulary of the French-Gothic style of construction. The exterior is of dressed stone and it has a cruciform floor plan. The interior was designed with a nave and two aisles, two side chapels, a high altar, two side altars, a vestry, a baptistery and a confessional. Over the high altar, is a restored tapestry of glass that depicts a

29

group of the crucifixion. A statue of Our Lady of Guadalupe presented by the people of Mexico was installed in the church on 10 October 1993.

When services are not on, the main door is often closed, but a side door on the right is kept open.

The original village of Shimla is regarded to have stood below St. Michael's Cathedral – in the present-day Ram Bazaar area.

Deputy Commissioner's Office and the Telegraph Office

Just above St. Michael's Cathedral are the offices of the Deputy Commissioner of the Shimla district. These are housed in a building where the crenellations of the main arch are done in the Norman baronial style of construction. Returning to the level of the Mall this walk ends at the Telegraph Office.

The brick and concrete structure of the Telegraph Office had one of the first 'automatic' telephone exchanges in India. The old Station Library once stood here, in a house called Conny Cot. The library was shifted in 1886, and a large wooden building was constructed in the Alpine chalet style to house the Telegraph Office. This was also demolished and the present building was completed in 1922 – amidst heavy criticism during the years of the First World War (1914 to 1918), over its expense.

The lower portion of the structure is a superb example of ashlar work – where each stone is shaped to be fitted in a specific position. In the original design, there were towers on the east and west ends, which were eliminated for economy at the time of actual construction. The foundations were elaborately wired to minimise the effects of seismic shocks. As you walk up from the

direction of St. Michael's Cathedral, i.e. from the west, you will see a cornerstone bearing the following statement in Latin: *Molem Aedificii Multi Construxerunt : Rationem Exegit I. Begg* (Many men created the stone work of this building : the work was directed by J. Begg.) J. Begg was one of Shimla's important architects. A section of the ground floor once used to hold a branch of the Lloyds Bank.

Diagonally opposite the Telegraph Office is what was the old Railway Booking Office and under the layers of signboards you can see its unusual character: its head resembles a steam locomotive turning a hill. You are now about a hundred metres from Scandal Point, where this walk began.

WALK TWO

Wide Sweeps of Greensward

The Glen and Annandale Walks.

The Glen Walk

From Scandal Point to the Glen which is a narrow
valley through which a stream flows.
This is more of a nature trail that goes to one of
Shimla's most popular picnic spots.

 DIRECTION, APPROXIMATE TIME AND DISTANCE

Up to Knockdrin, the route remains the same as in the one titled
'Where the White Man Carried his Burden'. At Knockdrin, the
fork leads down to the Glen. On a round trip, this walk covers
about seven to eight kilometres from Scandal Point. Plan for three
hours or longer.

 SUGGESTED TIME OF THE DAY

The best time to enjoy this walk is in the morning.

★ **HIGHLIGHTS**

Built heritage till Knockdrin.
The views, the trees, the little stream, the birds, and perhaps
some bees and butterflies while we are at it.

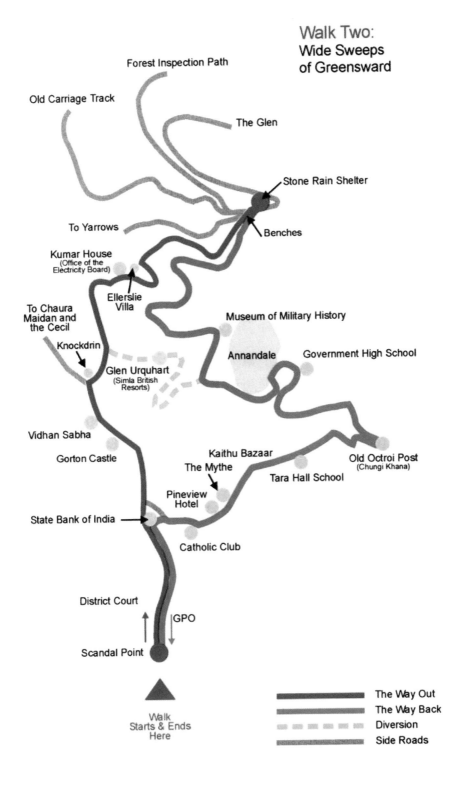

Walk Two:
Wide Sweeps
of Greensward

Forest Inspection Path

Old Carriage Track

The Glen

Stone Rain Shelter

Benches

To Yarrows

Kumar House
(Office of the
Electricity Board)

Ellerslie
Villa

To Chaura
Maidan and
the Cecil

Museum of Military History

Knockdrin

Glen Urquhart
(Simla British
Resorts)

Annandale

Government High School

Vidhan Sabha

Gorton Castle

Kaithu Bazaar

The Mythe

Old Octroi Post
(Chungi Khana)

Tara Hall School

Pineview
Hotel

State Bank of India

Catholic Club

District Court

GPO

Scandal Point

Walk
Starts & Ends
Here

The Way Out

The Way Back

Diversion

Side Roads

After Knockdrin

From the ARTRAC Mess at Knockdrin turn down right for the first part of this walk that is along the road to Annandale. There are a couple of attractive houses on this stretch and just by the road on the right are the offices of the Himachal Pradesh Khadi and Village Industries Board – marked by large signs in Hindi. Just ahead also on the right, below the road, is the turn that goes to the Simla British Resort; this road is a shortcut to Annandale. Ahead on the left, are the large offices of the Himachal Pradesh State Electricity Board at Kumar House. This is followed by Ellerslie Villa and Ellerslie Cottage. There is a small rain shelter on the right, opposite which a path goes up to the Government College for Boys at Kotshera House, the National Academy for Audit and Accounts and Yarrows. There are no real houses on the road till the Glen, after this shelter; other structures too are few, far between or distant.

The forested path

About two kilometres from the turn off at Knockdrin, at the point where the main road forms a horseshoe bend and cups a seating space, are the roads towards Glen and Annandale. While the main road continues down to Annandale, the path to the Glen branches off seeming almost like the tail of one of Shimla's famous monkeys. The marker for that path is a small stone shelter. At this point, narrow lanes also veer off to Yarrows; an old carriage track to Viceregal Lodge; and the narrow 'forest inspection trail' that finally circles Summer Hill (the university campus), some of whose structures can be seen from this point. If you wish to, you could take a short detour along the carriage track or the inspection trail and return by backtracking to this point. (These two are described below in the Annandale Walk.)

The views up to this point include glimpses of Annandale, the woods and aspects of two of Shimla's most majestic colonial structures – the accountant general's office at Gorton Castle and the present-day Vidhan Sabha. As one enters this narrow valley, expectedly the views also contract and focus on the flora and the stream.

Below the stone shelter is a small children's playground that someone decided must be protected by a stone wall (even if low), and topped by what may well be called mini-battlements. At the end of this fortress that protects the slides and swings, the path to the Glen turns off left, away from the side facing Annandale.

The path is well marked and will take you to a wooded ravine where several tiny brooks pour their water into a larger perennial stream. The first bit of the valley may leave you wondering why you bothered coming here at all – but cross the pumping station and much of the place's original character and beauty can be seen.

Where crinoline brushed the ferns

The Glen forms a part of a reserve forest and is one of Shimla's oldest and most popular picnic spots. *Thacker's New Guide to Simla* (1925) pronounced it as 'the "lion" of Simla's picnic places'. Cooed sweet nothings of couples were probably the loudest of roars here – unless it was the laughter of playing children. There are still a couple of concrete bins along the path that were placed an age ago to collect the garbage left behind by visitors.

The trees are representative of the region's flora and include oak, rhododendron, deodar (Himalayan cedar), and *chil* and *kail* pines. The broad-leaved varieties include horse-chestnut, cryptomeria and ash. The undergrowth is fairly luxuriant too. The birds and animals that may be sighted in the area – especially deep down in the valley – are pheasants, black partridges, yellow-throated martens, hen harriers, barking deer and if you are really lucky, then leopards, foxes and the leopard cat. The walk back is all uphill, so do try to return before sundown.

The area also has several narrow 'forest inspection trails' used by the staff of the forest department to check on the general well-being of the woods. These trails are regularly used by the trans-humant Gaddi tribe who move from pasture to pasture with their goats and sheep. There are several paths that lead down to the villages below the Glen that have been inhabited

long before even Shimla came into existence. If you are up to it, you can include Annandale (described ahead) in this walk.

Ferns, violets and snake plants

Some common wildflowers of Shimla are – aconite, anemones, asters, begonias, berberis, daisies, delphiniums, forget-me-nots, geraniums, gerberas, impatiens, iris, laburnum, lilies, marigolds, orchids, peonies, primulas, roses, sage, sedum, strawberries and violets.

The variety of ferns in the Shimla region is fairly substantial, and interestingly, as the common fern unfolds, it is sold as a vegetable locally called *lingru* – used to prepare a dish likened by some to asparagus, and is pickled as well. Meanwhile, the common violet has its own little claim to fame. Locally called *banaksha*, this is dried and used as a cure for sore throats; and combined with some other herbs (including the maidenhair fern) it makes the popular common cold palliative, Joshanda.

The snake plant, *Arisaema helleborifolium* can be treated as an index of the monsoon rains. It springs up as soon as the rains break in June-July and when its cob ripens and turns a deep red in September it announces the end of the monsoons. All though the wet months, it stands guard over the grasses like a hooded cobra, that gives it its name.

The Annandale Walk

From Scandal Point to Annandale past Kumar House;
the way back is through Lower Kaithu.

 DIRECTION, APPROXIMATE TIME AND DISTANCE

The first leg of the walk trail is up to Knockdrin and the second
leg is identical to the Glen walk up to the horseshoe bend. For
the third leg to reach Annandale, follow the metalled road all
through. This passes through thick deodar woods to reach a
large open glade. The walk towards Annandale is largely downhill
and all uphill on the return. From Scandal Point on the Mall,
this covers a distance of six to seven kilometres. Plan for three
hours or more.

The route may also be dovetailed with the Glen Walk
(described above), which will then take a total of around five
hours or more and will cover eight to twelve kilometres.

 SUGGESTED TIME OF THE DAY

The ideal time to go for this walk is in the morning.

★ **HIGHLIGHTS**

Built heritage up to Knockdrin
The woods and the views
The glade of Annandale
The Museum of Military History
Some old houses

39

Annandale

From the horseshoe bend mentioned in the Glen Walk, the tarmac road continues its steady descent through woods of cedar, oak, rhododendron and pine up to Annandale. This is the primary road.

The name 'Annandale' may have come from the valley with the same name in Dumfriesshire in Scotland; or, as another tradition maintains, from Anna, the lady who first visited the spot when the British began coming to Shimla. Annandale used to host fancy fairs, fetes, cricket and polo matches and also hold an extensive flower and fruit garden. The Annandale Gymkhana Club was one of the well known clubs of its time. It was here that the first plane landed in Shimla towards the end of the First World War. Regular horse races were held here till 1949. It was at Annandale that Lord Curzon, British Viceroy and Governor General of India (1899-1905) is said to have discussed with Sir Francis Younghusband the idea of a military expedition to Tibet, which reached its capital Lhasa in 1904. According to some sources, the idea of creating the Indian National Congress which came into being in 1885 and went on to spearhead the Freedom Movement was first discussed here by its founder, A.O. Hume.

Today, it has a museum of military history, a golf course and a helipad.

Just short of the glade is an attractive temple of wood and slate made in the local style of construction, and is a fairly representative example of the Shimla region's indigenous architecture. At certain times of the year, the images of some local deities like Gan Devta and Doomi Devta are carried from their primary temples in the neighbouring villages to 'meet' here.

The deodar woods give this walk much of its character. The

majestic Himalayan cedar (*cedrus deodara*) was not just a tree but also a god for the ancients. Its impressive form was an object of veneration and in all likelihood, the local name 'deodar' comes from *devdaru*, meaning 'a wood of the gods', or from *devtaru*, meaning 'like the gods'. Interestingly, there is also the belief in certain quarters that if a deodar tree is cut, out of greed or for no real purpose, it brings great misfortune to the person who has felled it, and may even take the life of someone within his household!

At this point, you can turn back or continue ahead; and through pockets of habitation take the steep climb via Kaithu up to the level of the Mall. Annandale is connected by a local bus service and you may opt for this as a return mode as well.

The climb up

If you continue, then go along the glade's right, and move past the club house and military museum. By the Nissen huts of corrugated iron sheets, where there is a Government High School, the road forms another horseshoe bend. Turn up. (A long hike that finally leads down to the river Satluj and Tattapani goes from this point via the village of Golcha.)

Past houses old and new, climb for some two hundred metres where there is an electricity transformer on the road. The road on the right goes up to a house named Gulab Kunj and reaches Upper Kaithu via the Police Lines, and then carries on to the level of the Mall. It is suggested that you go left in the direction of the old Chungi Khana, the one-time octroi post and Lower Kaithu, which will make the walk a little longer.

Another hundred metres or so is another crossroad. Again, the path on the right leads past some new concrete buildings up

to the Police Lines. A short detour down to the left takes you to a little park called the Gol Pahari, or Circular Hill that is nestled among pines and offers some lovely views of the area. The first ridge visible ahead is that of Elysium and the Bharari spur with the red brick of Auckland House School on a prominent display; this is followed by the spur of Mashobra and Naldehra while the high bare peak is the Shali, which at 3,200 metres is the highest in Shimla's vicinity.

The road to the Chungi Khana also lies on the left but is on the way up. Keep following the steady narrow road that climbs fairly remorselessly up to what are called the Pili Kothis, or Yellow Houses that were built in the 1940s with a bit of an eye on baroque curves for the roofline.

The large grey buildings that act as a steady beacon are those of the Convent at Tara Hall. Keep climbing past the Mythe and the Pineview Hotel to arrive a hundred metres higher at a bench under a large oak tree. Here, you could also take a short detour along the level road that moves left to Northbank, the one-time residence of Rudyard Kipling. Back on the climb, you go past the

gates of the one-time Catholic Club at Ensham Estate and the entrance of Fingask Estate, the one-time Chelmsford Club. (This bit features in the detour in the walk 'Where the White Man Carried his Burden'.) All through the climb, the views encompass the hills and the woods, while the snow-clad mountains pop up in snatches.

At this point, where the office of the Great Himalayan Travels and their carry-away food counter is located, you can take the staircase up to the temple of Kali Bari and reach Scandal Point. Or if the climbing has got a bit much, you can turn right and along the level road, reach the little cut that divides the house St. Mark's and the State Bank of India. Through this tiny pass, you will be at the Mall, where you turn left for Scandal Point.

The old carriage track

If at Annandale you decide to backtrack, then at the break off point towards the Glen, there are two rather inconspicuous unpaved paths on the hillside. When facing the hill, the path that rises sharply up arrives at a couple of old colonial residences, the Academy of the Indian Audit and Accounts Service, and Yarrows and brings you to the Mall near the Cecil. The path that hugs the outer edge of the hill brings you close to the gates of Indian Institute of Advanced Study. Both are interesting route variations but can be a little trying in patches due to the unwanted spillovers of human habitation. Interestingly, the latter path, which is largely a forest track, was the old carriage road taken by the viceroys for Annandale.

Some birds of Shimla

These woods have a fair bit of Shimla's bird life that includes pheasants, partridges, crows, sparrows, magpies, barbets, fowl, thrushes, tits, nuthatches, bulbuls, minivets, warblers, finches, woodpeckers and owls.

WALK THREE

Wishes on a Tree

From Scandal Point to the temple of Kamna Devi, atop
Prospect Hill, which is accessed from Boileauganj.

This walk also goes west from Scandal Point on the Mall. The approximate distance covered will be six to eight kilometres. Plan for at least two hours. Almost up to the gates of the Indian Institute of Advanced Study, the walk is identical to the one titled 'Where the White Man Carried his Burden'.

 SUGGESTED TIME OF THE DAY

This walk can be taken any time of day up to the early evening. Plan for morning or early afternoon if you wish to do the extensions as well.

★ HIGHLIGHTS

Built heritage
The views
Kamna Devi Temple

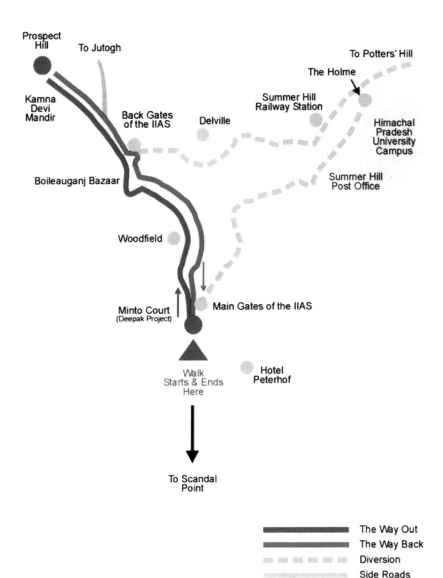

Walk Three:
Wishes on a Tree

Prospect Hill

To Jutogh

To Potters' Hill

The Holme

Kamna Devi Mandir

Summer Hill Railway Station

Back Gates of the IIAS

Delville

Himachal Pradesh University Campus

Boileauganj Bazaar

Summer Hill Post Office

Woodfield

Minto Court
(Deepak Project)

Main Gates of the IIAS

Walk Starts & Ends Here

Hotel Peterhof

To Scandal Point

The Way Out
The Way Back
Diversion
Side Roads

En route to the Boileauganj Bazaar

Just short of the gates of the Institute there is a road that branches off left at a slightly lower level than the main one. There is a rather fluctuating landmark in the shape of a small grocery store and STD telephone booth called the 'Deepika Veg & Grocery Shop, Project Deepak', and a more permanent one in the shape of the offices of the Deepak Project a few yards ahead. The Deepak Project is housed in a Tudor-framed structure that used to serve as the quarters of the viceregal band.

Continue along this road till you come to the Boileauganj Bazaar. En route you cross some attractive old houses, including the historically important, though rather tumble-down Woodfield. Nobel Laureate, and author of India's national anthem, 'Jana Gana Mana', the celebrated writer Rabindranath Tagore once stayed here.

Prospect Hill and the Temple of Kamna Devi

Boileauganj (locally pronounced 'Baloo-ganj'), is named after the Boileau bothers – one Captain J.T. Boileau had made the observatory on the hill above in 1840.

As you enter the bazaar, the police station is on your left. Cross both this and the fork that plunges down left immediately after. Keep walking and dodging the traffic for fifty yards or so. You will have crossed most of this small bazaar when you reach the spot where there are almost half a dozen large and small roads heading in different directions. Take the well defined steep slope up to the temple of Kamna Devi atop Prospect Hill, whose base is marked by a small unused guard post. The

Observatory House

climb is lined with many recently built houses and some old ones; the latter date back to the time when they used to be a part of the viceregal estate. Offering a magnificent view, this path is almost a kilometre long.

The hilltop is crowned by the temple of Kamna Devi – locally regarded as a goddess who grants wishes. Housing the deity, who is locally also called Kairaroo Devi, this is a single storeyed structure neatly done in brick. There is a small bush in the compound, the remnants of a *kainth* tree on which many tie a small red string and make a wish. The view from the top encompasses the valleys, distant mountains and has an interesting angle of the airport. If you have carried along a picnic snack, this makes a good point to take a breather and have a bite.

The return

From Kamna Devi you can return to the Mall. If you decide to do this, a route variation is suggested. At the bottom of the slope, by the bus stop's shelter, are the back gates of the Indian Institute of Advanced Study. Enter these, climb a little and then take the somewhat level road on the right that lies just above the bazaar and moves roughly parallel to the one that was used to reach Boileauganj. This road also arrives at the main gates of Institute of Advanced Study.

A little detour to the aviary, opposite the gates of the Institute, may be taken. Then, just to vary the route, at the level space with your back to the gates of the Institute, take the road on the left. This will also bring you to the base of the climb to the museum, close to the Cecil. On this track, the views of the northern hills are quite magnificent and if it is early spring, the rhododendrons will be in bloom.

Rhododendrons in bloom

The world-wide interest for rhododendrons was exported from India by the celebrated botanist, Sir Joseph Dalton Hooker who did most of his work away from Shimla, in the eastern parts of the country. The rhododendrons of Shimla, *rhododendron arboreum* grow to become trees unlike many of their cousins that are quite happy as bushes. Interestingly, Shimla's rhododendrons live cheek by jowl with the local oaks which in turn are quite unlike their relatives in other parts of the world and are fairly short and thin.

An option at Boileauganj

Another walk option lies at Boileauganj, on the return from the temple of Kamna Devi. You can walk on to the Himachal Pradesh University campus at Summer Hill and then to the gates of the Viceregal Lodge. This loop passing through woods of oak and rhododendron, with some fine views will add another two kilometres or so to the walk. From Summer Hill to the gates of the Viceregal Lodge, the road lies just above the railway track.

And another option at Summer Hill

Summer Hill holds yet another option. This is also the point where you carry on to the woods of the Conservation Zone called Van Vihar, to Potters' Hill and to the rain-fed Chadwick Falls. While this is given as a separate walk entitled 'To Rain-fed Falls', if you are a keen walker you can include it in this walk as well. If you do, the following is the route to take.

There is a road that lies just above the Summer Hill railway station. Continue along this till you arrive at the Conservation Zone and Potters' Hill. The way is over a tarmac road and is quite well marked. In the Conservation Zone you may be able see a variety of butterflies. Potters' Hill has a camp where you can get a good meal or snack.

If you have taken the entire route from Scandal Point to Boileauganj to Kamna Devi to Summer Hill to the Conservation Zone and back to Scandal Point, you will cover approximately ten to twelve kilometres. The walk is along level stretches and mild slopes – barring the sharp half-kilometre climb to the temple of Kamna Devi. Plan for at least six hours.

En route, Summer Hill has two historically important houses: The Holme, once the residence of the celebrated artist Amrita Shergil and Manorville, the property of Rajkumari Amrit Kaur, where Mahatma Gandhi often stayed. Both Boileauganj and Summer Hill have some simple eating places.

▲ *In winter, a stretch down to the Mall from the Ridge.*

The Ridge after a light snowfall. ▼

A Swiss Bavarian style window at the Cooper Block of the Cecil.

Maria Brothers. Shimla's famous antiquarian bookstore on the Mall.

The Mall, with the municipal offices on the left and the Gaiety Theatre complex ahead.

◀ *Our Lady of Guadalupe at St. Michael's Cathedral.*

▼ *One of Chapslee's bedrooms.*

Gorton Castle behind snow-flecked cedar trees. ▼

▲ *Wild strawberries.*

Wild raspberries. ▶

◀ *Bantony Annexe.*

The road to Viceregal Lodge.

The back lawns and Viceregal Lodge. ▼

Stone staircase that leads to the back terraces of Viceregal Lodge.

(facing page):
Blooms outside Viceregal Lodge.
▲ ▼
The public entry wing of Viceregal Lodge.

Begonias in bloom at the glasshouse of Viceregal Lodge. ▼

Viceregal Lodge, now the Indian Institute of Advanced Study. ▼

▲
Moss covered rocks and the little stream at the Glen.

Rhododendrons in bloom, still a common sight around Shimla in spring. ▶

WALK FOUR

To Rain-fed Falls

From Scandal Point to Chadwick Falls and back
through Summer Hill after a glimpse of Potters' Hill.

Chadwick Falls – that everyone includes in his or her itinerary but never gets around to visiting – lie in the western edges of Shimla, as does Potters' Hill. This is a long walk and if you intend using your legs all the way from Scandal Point and back, plan for five to six hours or more. You will cover between twelve to fifteen kilometres along slopes and level stretches. The last leg of two kilometres or so is along a narrow path in a forest.

SUGGESTED TIME OF THE DAY

A morning departure is suggested so that you are at the Falls by midday or early afternoon.

★ HIGHLIGHTS

Built heritage up to the former Viceregal Lodge
Summer Hill
The woods and views
Chadwick Falls
Potters' Hill
Summer Hill Railway Station
Boileauganj (if included as a route extension)
Prospect Hill and the temple of Kamna Devi
    (if included as a route extension)

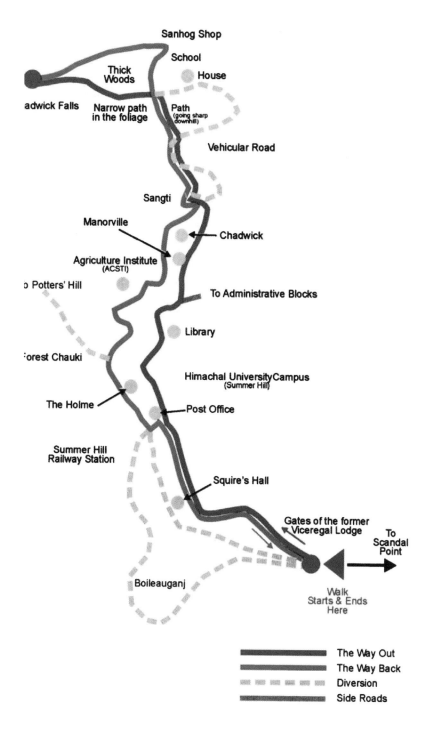

Three routes half-way to Chadwick Falls

 Up to the gates of the Institute of Advanced Study, this walk remains the same as the one titled 'Where the White Man Carried his Burden'. At this point you can take any of the following three routes to the campus of the Himachal Pradesh University at Summer Hill, the starting point for the track to Chadwick Falls.

The shortest is the direct route to the university from Scandal Point or the Mall. At the gates of the Indian Institute of Advanced Study take the fork that lies on the right hand side of the gates. Between the gates of the Institute and Summer Hill, the road is about a kilometre long and passes under trees of cedar, oak and rhododendron. The hillside is covered with a variety of ferns and grasses. A section of this runs just above the railway track. The views include the upper reaches of the Glen, the Bharari spur and the snow peaks.

Somewhat longer (one and a half kilometres), is the route that moves roughly parallel to this and lies about a hundred metres higher up the hill. To take this route, enter the gates and walk up towards the Institute's building. About fifty metres short of the building, on the climb itself, there is a fork that holds a narrow and largely level road to the right. There is (usually) a bench here. This leads to Squire's Hall, a part of the old viceregal estate and today, the residence of the director of the Indian Institute of Advanced Study. By the gates of the Hall, the road takes a slope down which leads to Summer Hill. This is road that sees negligible vehicular traffic and pedestrians are also few and far between. It passes through woods of oak and rhododendron and offers a good view of the valleys and mountains. The first valley below is the one that holds the Glen. A warning though, every once in a while the road is closed off near the university and there may be just a few strands of barbed wire to greet you at the end. (The guard at the main gates of the Institute *might* be able to tell you if the gates towards the university side are open.)

The longest route is via Boileauganj and is described in the walk to Prospect Hill. The section used for this walk is the same as in that one, up to Summer Hill – skipping the climb to the temple of Kamna Devi. For all practical purposes, this walk loops around the entire hill which holds the viceregal estate. From the gates of the Institute up to Summer Hill, this will cover about three and a half kilometres.

From Summer Hill Post Office

Suitably decorated by graffiti, the Post Office of Summer Hill is a pretty little building (or what can be seen of it) with pebbledash walls that stands at the head of a short stone staircase. The walk route climbs up on the right of this into the campus of the Himachal Pradesh University. Near the top of the climb, is another

one of Shimla's newer space travel inspired buildings; this one is the university library that looks like a bloated version of an Apollo series moon landing craft. Take a moment to step to the other side of this wonder and you will be able to view Shimla town, especially a section of its northern slopes, from an unusual angle. Back on the road, and another hundred metres or so, there is a fork on the left with a somewhat downhill incline towards the village of Sangti, also called Shangti; somewhat following the Simla-Shimla routine.

Manorville and ahead

Here, the first house on the left is called Manorville, which was the property Rajkumari Amrit Kaur (1889-1964), daughter of Raja Sir Harnam Singh of Kapurthala. In the struggle for India's freedom, she was a close associate of Mahatma Gandhi – who often stayed here while visiting Shimla. She was India's first woman cabinet minister. The All India Institute of Medical Sciences was created at the initiative of Prime Minister Jawaharlal Nehru and her. She then donated this rather eclectic brick and timber house to the Indian Council of Medical Sciences.

The road continues moving steadily down through woods of oak and rhododendron, and the views to the north are magnificent – the snow ranges are visible on a clear day. On the right now comes the newly made HPU Faculty House. Just ahead, on the left, in a gated area and surrounded by apartment blocks, is Chadwick House that is one of the town's 'see it while you can' structures. Tired, crumbling and abandoned, this was built by General G.F.L. Marshall in the 1880s and then passed into the hands of Raja Charanjit Singh of Kapurthala. Of its once-legendary garden, there is no trace.

Towards the Falls

The walk route goes right, from the gates of Chadwick House, and continues its descent to Sangti. Just short of the buildings that make the village of Sangti, there is a branch off path, somewhat like a horseshoe bend. This continues down to the village of Sanhog and may be followed on this walk, though a shortcut may be taken here from Sangti. The straight road followed so far continues on to circle Summer Hill and arrives back at the Post Office.

At Sangti, the shortcut moves right of the small temple dedicated to Devi Durga. This continues down to meet the road. Turn left and take the next bend along the road. Just after this bend, a path with stone soling again cuts down on the left and will meet the road some three hundred metres lower down.

Into the woods

Right here, on the left again and towards the inner parts of the hill, somewhat screened by brambles, a narrow path turns down.

This is the one that leads to Chadwick Falls.

An alternative route can be taken from here. If at this point you have some doubts about the turn off to the Falls, carry on down the vehicular road for another half a kilometre or so till you reach the village of Sanhog. On the road itself and near each other, are a school building and a small shop. A path to the Falls, again on the left, goes from here.

If you have kept to the path mentioned earlier, you will be taking a largely downward slope with a few level patches. It is fairly narrow with its width rarely exceeding two feet, but it is well defined. The forest is quite dense and has oak, rhododendron, pine and cedar trees – with the usual accompaniment of ferns, grasses and wildflowers. This path carries on for about a kilometre till you reach the Falls.

Chadwick Falls

That a Mister or Colonel Chadwick after whom the houses mentioned and the Falls are supposedly named, ever existed has not been established till date. Be that as it may, the Falls are an impressive sight during the monsoons even if they are nothing but a trickle through the rest of the year. Surrounded by thick woods, they are about sixty metres high and pour their waters into a small pool – which is used by the few animals that remain in the area to quench their thirst. There is also a small rain shelter near the Falls.

And then out of the woods

For the way back, take the lower path that was offered as the alternative route for coming. This is more level and is simply another path to check out. This arrives opposite the shop and the school in the village of Sanhog. In the pines of Sanhog, there is a small enclosure dedicated to the local deity, Gan Devta.

From here, backtrack up to Sangti. Once you are back on the main road by the Durga temple, from where you started the sharp descent, turn right. This is the road that circles Summer Hill and again the woods are a combination of oak, rhododendron, cedar and pine, with a few horse-chestnuts and holly tossed in for good measure. On the right, en route, are buildings that belong to The Agriculture Co-operative Staff Training Institute of the H.P. State Co-operative Bank Ltd. – that apart from the long-winded name, serve as a good route marker.

About one and a half kilometres from Sangti there is a crossing. Clearly marked, a road here turns right for Potters' Hill.

Potters' Hill

The road to Potters' Hill turns off here and goes by the Summer Hill Police Post and the university's boys' hostel. Potters' Hill was so named after the large number of potters who lived and made clay pottery in the area. The potters, who came into town carrying flower pots and pitchers in bags of woven hemp, were gradually pushed into professions by a dwindling market. The presence of a camp also named Potters' Hill has reinforced this old identity. Apart from the camp, this area has good woods of primarily pine, oak and rhododendron and there is also a small gallery of photographs with an excellent display of Himachal's landscapes, people and culture.

The way back

If you've not turned to Potters' Hill, then the road turning up or the level one at the fork will take you in the direction of the Summer Hill Post Office. (The one that goes sharply down, goes to a village named Sheli.) At the fork, the level one is suggested for this walk. This is a quieter road and a short distance ahead, on the left and above the road are two houses with pebbledash walls, The Holme and The Studio. These were once the property of Umrao Singh Shergil whose famous daughter, Amrita did a significant part of her painting here and went on to exercise a powerful influence over modern Indian art.

On the right below with neat gables is the Summer Hill railway station on the regular Kalka-Shimla railway line. This is the station just before Shimla and was often used by the viceroys – as the Lodge lay just above. Here again, you have a few options to choose from.

You can take a train back, if the timing is right. The ride will take around ten minutes.

Another is to walk back along the railway track. If you choose to do this, do check the timings of incoming and outgoing trains at the station. There are a couple of tunnels en route and No. 103 (called the Inverarm tunnel, which is just short of Shimla) is 350 metres long and while there are nooks in between to shelter in, it is best to be aware of this. The distance between Summer Hill railway station and the one at Shimla is about 2.6 kilometres and between Shimla station and Scandal Point, is about 1.5 kilometres. This walk can give a sample of some of the heritage of the railway track and the route is through woods of oak, rhododendron and cedar.

You can take a bus back from the stop near the Post Office which lies about a hundred metres above the station. Get off at the A.G. Office bus stop (this is at Gorton Castle) or at the main bus stand. From either, you can walk up to the Mall and Scandal Point.

And the following three routes will take you to the gates of the Institute.

Walk along the road just above the Summer Hill railway station to Boileauganj, and backtrack along the route mentioned at the start of this walk.

Or, with your back to the Summer Hill Post Office, on the right and ahead, there is a narrow road going up (the wide one going down goes to Boileauganj). This goes past Squire's Hall and arrives at the gates of the Institute, if the gates of the Hall are open.

Walk from the Summer Hill Post Office on the road left. This is the shortest route back to the gates of the Institute. From here, you can walk back to the Mall and Scandal Point.

The Kalka-Shimla Railway Line

Of the many stories told along the Kalka-Shimla railway line, there is perhaps none as fascinating as that of Bhalku, a labourer who worked on the track. The tale goes that he had long matted hair that were infested with lice – which he used to feed by pouring sugar and flour over his head. He claimed that the trace the line should take had been revealed to him by his *deuta* who communicated with him through the lice. Trailed by the engineers and their theodolites and plane tables, he would march with a long staff over the hills and it is said that even H.S. Harington, Agent of the Railway was in awe of Bhalku's 'supernatural' powers and always deferred to him. The Kalka-Shimla railway line is supposed to have been built on exactly the trace 'revealed' by Bhalku.

It was on 9 November 1903 that the line was opened to traffic as a link from the Delhi-Ambala-Kalka branch of the East Indian Railway and covered some ninety-five kilometres of mountainous terrain. The broad gauge line and the puffing giants ended at Kalka and then, littler locomotives and 'toy carriages' took the thirty-inch gauge.

Initially, there were 107 tunnels and today, there are a 102. For tradition's sake, the line is still referred to have a 103 tunnels – the figure it had for most of its life, but Number 46 (that was at the Solan Brewery) is no longer there. There are eight hundred bridges and nine hundred curves and during its course through the picturesque countryside that characterises the lower reaches of the Himalaya, the line sometimes goes through a succession of reverse curves of over thirty-six metres radii. The bridges that resemble Roman aqueducts are replete with building skills and the longest arch viaduct has an aggregate length of 2.8 kilometres. The railway was purchased by the state in 1906 and had cost Rs 17,107,748 at the time of its construction.

WALK FIVE

Heritage Miles

From the Telegraph Office,
via the Mall to Barnes' Court and
then back to the Ridge over the Forest Hill Road.

DIRECTION, APPROXIMATE TIME AND DISTANCE

This walk goes from the shopping area of the Mall and loops back to the Ridge via Barnes' Court (or Raj Bhavan, the official residence of the state governor), the Forest Hill Road (also called "Lovers' Lane") and the Ramchandra Chowk. This walk covers five to six kilometres along fairly level stretches as well as slopes. Plan for two hours or more.

SUGGESTED TIME OF THE DAY

Anytime of the day is good for this walk, barring late evening.

⭐ HIGHLIGHTS

Built heritage, the views and the trees
The Mall
The Gaiety Theatre
Oakover and The Cedars
Woodville and Barnes' Court
U.S. Club (United Services Club)
Christ Church
The Ridge

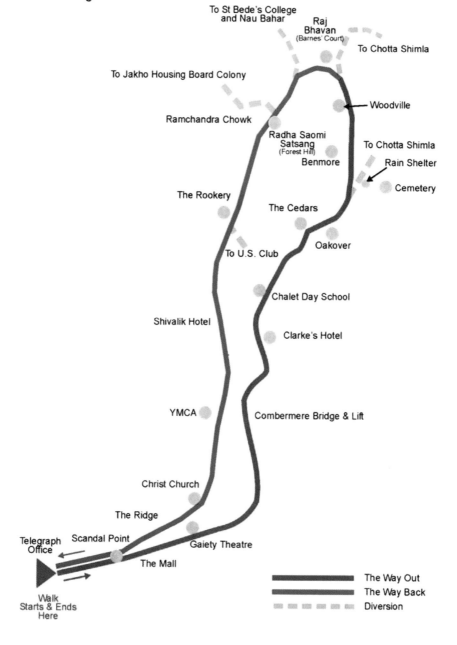

Walk Five:
Heritage Miles

To St Bede's College
and Nau Bahar

Raj
Bhavan
(Barnes' Court)

To Chotta Shimla

To Jakho Housing Board Colony

Woodville

Ramchandra Chowk

Radha Saomi
Satsang
(Forest Hill)

To Chotta Shimla

Rain Shelter

Benmore

Cemetery

The Rookery

The Cedars

Oakover

To U.S. Club

Chalet Day School

Shivalik Hotel

Clarke's Hotel

YMCA

Combermere Bridge & Lift

Christ Church

The Ridge

Telegraph
Office

Scandal Point

Gaiety Theatre

The Mall

The Way Out

The Way Back

Diversion

Walk
Starts & Ends
Here

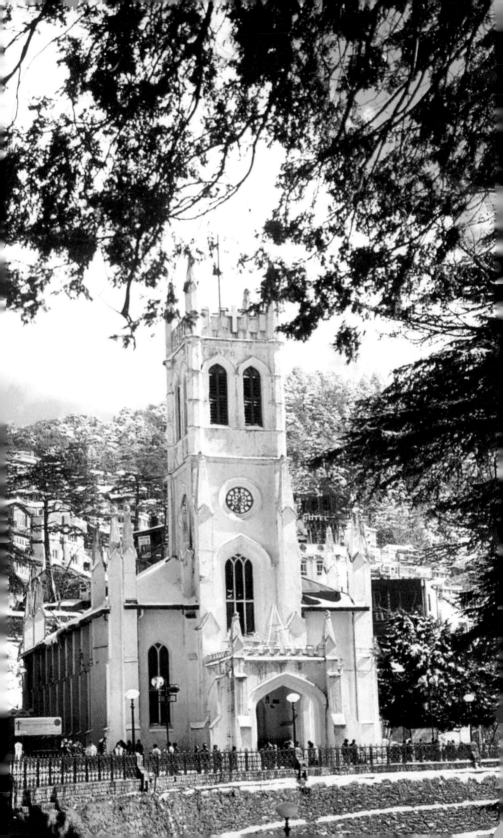

The Telegraph Office

The starting point for the Mall's row of shops (which expectedly changed hands and names every few years), is the lower section of Telegraph Office. Opposite this is the building that loosely resembles a steam locomotive – which it may as well because till very recently, it was the Railway Booking Office. The shops, banks and offices of this pedestrian stretch now begin and are often likened to a marketplace in rural England. The Mall forms the core of the declared Heritage Zone of Shimla and its alignment follows what was perhaps the first road to be built in town.

Some Shop Architecture

Walking slowly along this stretch will reveal a range of architectural details of the older buildings. For example, there is much variety to be found in the different settings of stone or brick.

Near the start of the Mall is the present-day Himachal Emporium whose premises once housed the tailor A.E. Jones. Jones was a brilliant amateur ornithologist who prepared a fine booklet on the birds of Shimla. Nearby, today's Davico's and Coffee Day restaurant used to hold the well-known grocers Spencer and Co. Small details like the variation of columns and windows have added an enormous amount of character to the stretch. There are little architectural idiosyncrasies too – the windows on the floor above the Indian Coffee House hold conventional bay windows in lotus-inspired cupolas; and on the

ground-floor, Mr Framjee once sold the finest of liquors and wines. The structure that now looks like a rather grand public facility, the Jankidas Building once held the fine store by that name, where earlier, Whiteaway, Laidlaw and Company used to have their shop. In a large, pillar-free hall the first floor held the 'almost legendary' restaurant, The Davico's, initially run by the Davico brothers.

The Northbrook Terrace that now holds the Syndicate Bank and the Playworld Video Game Parlour, is regarded to have held the earliest of Shimla's stores. At this point, you are just below the General Post Office.

The Gaiety Theatre

Ahead, the space where the roads to the Ridge, the Mall and the General Post Office meet is called Scandal Point. This remains the hub of Shimla's social life till date. A statue of Lala Lajpat Rai, Punjab's nationalist leader who died in 1928 was brought from Lahore and re-erected at this spot; it is believed that the raised finger was broken in transit and redone.

Continue past the fire station, on your left lies the dressed-stone structure of the Municipal Corporation and just ahead is the famous Gaiety Theatre. The first recorded amateur dramatic performance in Shimla was on 9 June 1838 – and it was not an easy one. A member of the cast who was to act the woman's role, refused to cut off his moustache, while another decided that the time was ripe to go bear hunting.

The cast was replaced and the play took place in what the Lord Auckland's sister Emily Eden described in 1838 as '. . . a little sort of theatre . . . small and hot and somewhat dirty'. This would probably have been in the old Assembly Rooms in the area of today's *subzi mandi*, the vegetable market. From that day on, dramatics, the Amateur Dramatic Club and the Gaiety Theatre have played a major role in Shimla's social and cultural life; though the Amateur Dramatic Club was formally housed in the Gaiety Theatre only in 1887. This building, which was the old Town Hall, was completed on 30 May 1887. It then had a basement and four floors above ground level. Essentially Gothic in style, the architect was Henry Irwin (who also built Viceregal Lodge and the Ripon Hospital), and the structure completely dominated Shimla's skyline and southern slopes. It then held all the following – theatre, Masonic hall, municipal offices, police station, gallery of the theatre, bar-room, station library, a voluntary armoury, ballroom, retiring and drawing rooms and cloakrooms – and the tower was designed to house the volunteer adjutant's office and a room for meteorological observations. Major defects in the building – largely caused by the stone used – were noticed soon after its completion. For safety, in 1911, the upper portions of the building were dismantled. Subsequently, some minor additions were made to the remains of this once huge edifice; which have also been removed for the restoration that gives the structure much of its original grandeur. A concrete band marks the line above which all the work is new.

The Gaiety Theatre is renowned for its fine acoustics – and without the aid of an amplifier, a whisper on the stage will carry to every corner of the hall. This was built after a design that won the prize offered by the Dramatic Society of London. Electric lighting replaced gas in 1896 and at one point, Gaiety's wardrobe and props were regarded as among the finest in the world. The celebrated writer, Rudyard Kipling, the founder of the Boy Scout Movement, R. Baden-Powell, the renowned artist, Amrita Shergil and the Kendalls have all acted on Gaiety's stage. The great singer, K.L. Saigal is believed to have given his first public performance here. Several contemporary Indian actors have also appeared on its stage.

And some more bits of architecture

Past the Gaiety Theatre, the building of the Khadi Gram Udyog with its elaborate woodwork is of interest and it once housed the Empire Stores. The space open to the valley by the side of this building shows a part of the Lower Bazaar and the valley below. Across, on the first row of hills lies the temple of Tara Devi and past this is Kasauli. A small section of Solan is also visible as is Subathu in the dip. Needless to say, their lights do look rather pretty at night. Further down the Mall, just short of the lift and now largely obscured by fresh construction, is Combermere Bridge.

Combermere Bridge

Combermere Bridge was named after General Stapleton, the Viscount Combermere and the British Commander-in-Chief of the Indian Army from 1825. He personally oversaw its full construction. It was built in 1828 and along with the road, it was the first major work of a public nature in Shimla. Spanning a deep ravine, it connected the lower parts of Jakho hill and the area of Chotta Shimla. Originally built of wood by local craftsmen largely using local techniques, this was subsequently reconstructed. Surrounded by a thick forest, a water tank was also built here at that time. This was located where another one of Shimla's spaceship-inspired structures, the Games Complex prepares itself for takeoff. The streams feeding the tank were later supplemented by tunnels that were bored a short distance into the hill. This was as the first somewhat permanent source of water for the residents of Shimla.

Regent House lies just after the Lift and its first floor held the famous Peliti's Restaurant – alluded to by Rudyard Kipling. The Cavalier Peliti came from a village near Turin, Italy and is credited with having popularised western style confectionery in India. He was also a brilliant photographer who created a remarkable record of Shimla and other parts of India in the late nineteenth century.

Then comes the half-timbered structure of the Clarke's Hotel.

Ernest Clarke's loan

The Clarke's may not be one of the fancier hotels of Shimla and may well be at the lower end of the long list of properties that the Oberoi chain of hotels has, but its doors bear the origins of one of the great success stories of modern India.

In the history of Indian hotels, the story of the Clarke's Hotel begins in the 1920s when it was still called the Carlton. This was when Ernest Clarke arrived as the manager of the Cecil that lay at the other end of the Mall. At the Cecil, there was a college dropout working as a desk clerk at a salary of Rs 60 a month. His name was Mohan Singh Oberoi. Both Ernest and his wife Gertrude took a liking to the hard working young man. A while after Clarke had been at the Cecil, he asked the youth, 'I have rented the Carlton Hotel. Would you like to come with me?'

For a brief moment Oberoi looked up from the ledger. 'Yes, thank you,' he replied. At the Carlton, Oberoi became a jack of all trades – manager, clerk, and storekeeper rolled into a dapper frame. And at the end of the month, he found that he carried home a substantial Rs 15 more than what he used to at the Cecil. Four of Shimla's packed years swirled past the doors of the Carlton when both Ernest and Gertrude decided to go home for a while. In their six month absence, Mohan Singh was left in charge. Within that period, all due to the young man's enterprise, the hotel's occupancy increased up to eighty percent and profits shot up. Mohan Singh and his wife, Issar Devi themselves went to buy the vegetables and meat – knocking a solid fifty percent off the normal kitchen bill.

Ernest Clarke returned to Shimla and a short four months later, decided to permanently return to England. He offered the hotel to his tutelary genius. Oberoi did not have the Rs 25,000 that the shares were worth and asked for some time to raise the amount. Ernest Clarke, the story goes, smiled, and said, 'Send it to my London address whenever you can.' That was in 1934. Five years later, the interest-free loan had been repaid and the rest, as the cliché goes, is history.

After the Clarke's is the Day School at the Chalet. The name is indicative of its architectural style and this was once a part of the United Services Club. This was the only portion of the Club where its all male members could entertain lady guests and was better known in town as the 'hen house'. On the right, is the Simla Club and as its rotunda-like structure indicates that this was the bandstand below what were the open balconies of the Chalet. Just off this walk route, below the Simla Club are the brick Bemloe Cottages with touches of Edwardian architecture that were built for European officers stationed in town and completed in 1922.

Houses and some more

The colonial bungalow was already an evolved residential form by the time it arrived in Shimla. The typical one was built on a single level on a standard floor plan. There was porch or verandah – or both. Then came the entrance hall, with the drawing room on one side and the dining on the other, while the bedrooms were at the back. Where the house was double-storeyed, the bedrooms moved upstairs. Dimensions, or the addition and location of a study or morning room, maybe a billiards room or a library, were the only real variations.

Kitchens and their smoking fireplaces were often relegated to outhouses, reached by a covered passageway connected to the pantry. Given the lavishness of the colonial lifestyle, the number of servants was considerable: a dozen or more were attached to any 'ordinary' household and the system functioned reasonably well. In later years, the outdoor kitchen moved in, and it is interesting to see a house that has rooms of huge proportions and is blessed with only a postage stamp-sized kitchen; often a converted pantry.

71

Adjuncts to the main house were rows of servants' quarters, a rickshaw garage, stables and the occasional cowshed.

Apart from the bungalows, there also were shop-houses, flats and littler cottages. While *dhajji* remained the most popular form of construction, it was by no means the only one. Locally available stone and brick were also used, as were walls of planks and rammed earth. Many of the later houses of colonial Shimla were built in concrete and brick and often the floors were over-layered with planks or wooden tiles.

While the interior of every house was inevitably different, ranging from the Spartan bare-minimum that characterised people on the move, to the richly elaborate, it is the external ornamentation – both practical and decorative – that is worth a moment's pause. Gables with finials and decorated eaves boards and dormer windows break the monotony of the rooflines. Many of the long, low houses have their deep eaves and canopies elaborately adorned. One of the more remarkable embellishments is of the finely turned and corbelled features that are seen on Alpine chalets. Valances on south-facing windows and verandahs were seldom plain; if they did not have jewel-like tasselled fringes, they were in the very least, modestly fret-worked. Gothic-revival occasionally popped up on voussoired windows, and Doric or Corinthian columns on porches and even by windows took the place of simple wooden members. Balusters and engrailed arches covered whole ranges of design.

Windows were richly varied. While the bay window – often acting as a door to the verandah or terrace – was very popular, there are numerous examples of the standard sash window and even of Venetian and Georgian ones. Glass panes and art deco stained glass were used in all sorts of patterns, and the diamond cut was fairly popular.

In Shimla, indigenous elements were merged into an eclectic blend with the architectural experience of the west. It is only a rare house that adheres to the strict norms of a category, and it is a rarer one that does not employ myriad forms. Many of history's great edifices are often seen as a bid to establish permanence in a transient world. The grandiose monuments of the British Empire seem to reinforce this belief. Though not completely devoid of imperial overtones, the houses, at least, are more personal, more friendly, and more communicative. Today, what remains of these houses stands witness to an extraordinary historical episode and provides a remarkable insight into a way of life that has vanished.

Oakover and The Cedars

Ahead, you will see another fine example of the Swiss Bavarian style with ornate woodwork and filigreed metal in The Cedars. On the right is Oakover, the official residence of the chief minister of Himachal Pradesh and once the property of the Maharaja of Patiala. Just past this, by the rain-shelter is Shimla's oldest Christian cemetery. This burial ground was opened about 1828 and the first grave is dated 1829. As the town started growing, it was found to be too close to habitation and was closed; the last grave is of Captain Mathew Ford and is dated 17 March 1841. This cemetery has about a dozen graves and monuments.

Benmore, Woodville and Raj Bhavan (Barnes' Court)

Just after Oakover, the walk route turns left towards Woodville and the Raj Bhavan. Short of Woodville is Benmore. The original house was built around 1850. In 1863, this passed into the hands of Major Innes who the sold it to Felix von Goldstein, a leading estate agent of Shimla. Several improvements were made to the property by Goldstein and as a club and the property of his Simla Rink Company Limited, this became a focus of the town's social life; and sure enough, it finds mention in the writings of Rudyard Kipling. In 1885, this was purchased by the Punjab government who placed their offices in the main house while its secretariat was being built at Chotta Shimla, and even after that, Benmore retained its role in housing various offices.

The secretariat pops up for brief glimpses along this walk. Work on the building began in 1899 on a design by Lieutenant Colonel H.E.S. Abbott of the Royal Engineers. Locally quarried stone, concrete and iron were liberally used in the structure that was completed in 1902 and the Punjab government occupied this for the summer months. In 1967, this was taken over by the government of Himachal Pradesh.

Next, up on the left is Woodville, a stately art deco mansion which now functions as a 'heritage hotel'. Beginning with General Sir William Rose Mansfield in 1865, Woodville served as the residence of four successive commanders-in-chief of the Indian Army for the following decade. In 1881, this passed into the hands of one of Shimla's leading citizens, Sir James Walker and then became the residence of the managers of the Alliance Bank of Simla. The Bank collapsed in 1923 and in 1926, Woodville was bought by the ruler of the former princely state of Gondal, Sir Bhagvat Singh for his daughter, Leila. In 1938, the old house was pulled down by Leila's husband, Raja Sir Bhagat Chand of Jubbal, and this art deco mansion was built.

Raj Bhavan is the residence of the governor of Himachal Pradesh. Earlier called Barnes' Court, Raj Bhavan's handsome neo-Tudor building was the residence of various commanders-in-chief and then, the governors of the Punjab. It was here that the news of the Great Uprising of 1857 was given to General Anson. The historic Simla Agreement between India and Pakistan was signed here on 3 July 1972.

Most of the building is shielded from view by high gates and metal louvers. The trench-like road on the left is the walk route that rises past Raj Bhavan and climbs to the old Forest Hill Road – the one-time Lovers' Lane. This road climbs with the P.W.D. Rest House below the road on your right and the offices of the Lokayukta above on the left and a couple of hundred yards later, you are at the upper gates of the Raj Bhavan and the Forest Hill Road.

Some business of name-calling

India's British rulers often compared the landscape of Shimla to the highlands of Scotland. Several names and words from Scotland find corners in Shimla – Glengarry or Craig Dhu. Benmore probably derived its name from the same place in Dunoon Argyll, Scotland. And while the English, the Irish and the Scots all combined to rule India, there remained a fair amount of leg-pulling among the three. The Scots took digs at the Irish and the English had their little bits to say of both.

An interesting example is in the number of names which hark back to Scot nationalism and their fights against the English. The story of Sir William Wallace (c. 1274-1305) and the places connected with his life and struggle against the English, appear in several place-names. Wallace had his castle at Ellerslie which in Shimla gave its name to the former secretariat of the Punjab government; this now houses the secretariat of Himachal Pradesh. Stirling was regarded as the gateway to the north, where some frenzied parleys and complicated intrigues took place, and in Shimla, Stirling Castle occupies a rise on the town's northern aspect. Robert 'The Competitor' Bruce who was able to wrest the Scottish crown from England, was the Fifth Lord of Annandale, a valley in Dumfriesshire and where Wallace gathered many of the highland clans in their battle against Edward 'Longshanks' I, the

Plantagenet King of England. Shimla's Annandale was probably named after this and today, this concourse has a helipad and golf course. The Earl of Bothwell was one the many who died fighting by Wallace's side. Shimla's Bothwell Lodge lies close to Snowdon.

The Forest Hill Road

With your back to the gate, the turn to the right will take you to St. Bede's College, the Convent of Jesus and Mary, Nau Bahar and on to Sanjauli. For a long time, the locals called the Convent of Jesus and Mary 'Pun-yeer School'. The site had held the Pioneer Lines and the regiment of Pioneers was largely responsible for building the original Hindustan Tibet Road. The walk can continue to the Sanjauli Chowk, where you turn left towards the Government College. This track will bring you back to the Ridge and the Mall via Lakkar Bazaar. This forms a part of the walk described separately as 'The Jakho Round'.

This walk, however, turns left above Raj Bhavan and you cross the Ramchandra Chowk (named after one of Shimla's leading citizens and a distinguished civil servant). The old house, Forest Hill that belonged to the Ramchandras has been pulled down and replaced by the Radha Saomi Satsang.

An option at Ramchandra Chowk is to take the fork right and climb the hill through the Housing Board Colony to reach the Hanuman temple atop Jakho. Or short of the temple turn towards the Titla Hotel. (The latter bit is part of the walk titled 'The Jakho Round'.)

On this route, you can carry on along the level track past the policeman's box and watch the town unfold below.

Another kilometre ahead, you can choose two routes to return to the Mall.

Forming a sharp slope just past the house called The Rookery, the road drops down to the Mall and cuts through the old United Services Club to reach the Mall near the Lift. The recommended road carries on to the Ridge.

The U.S. Club

The buildings of the former United Services Club rest on a site that originally held a house named The Priory. In 1862, this house passed into the hands of a joint-stock company known as the Simla Club and North-West Wine Company. The Club obtained this in 1866 and developed the estate as residences of members of the services who were on temporary postings and short stays in Shimla. Over the subsequent years, the buildings were expanded to include the Club House, a Library, a court for 'Canadian' tennis, apartments, stables and accommodation for the staff and the Club officials. The membership of the Club was unlimited, though this was largely confined to the civil and military wings of the Government and the ecclesiastical establishment. The former Club House now has the offices of the Public Works Department and once held the dining hall and the reading, reception, writing, billiard and card rooms.

When the partition of India and the creation of Pakistan was being chalked out in 1947, the Boundary Commission that was to determine the borders, held many of its sittings here. The unverifiable story is also told of the draftsman who was given the task of drawing the actual lines on the map. This he would do in one of the residential apartments of the U.S. Club – drinking, crying and mumbling through the night.

The Ridge

The Ridge holds Christ Church which was consecrated in 1857, is quite the signature along the town's skyline. This is embellished with some fine stained glass and memorial tablets while pews still mark the seats of the British viceroy of India, the commander-in-chief and the governor of the Punjab. By the side of the church is the neo-Tudor structure of the Library.

The Ridge is still the widest open space in central Shimla and has long been a hub of the town's activity, and the town's main water tanks are encased just below the tarmac. Before Independence, this was where the king's birthday parades were held, and for many years this was the venue for political rallies. Even today, this remains a centre of leisure and is popular for its balloon sellers, ice-cream stalls and horse rides.

Shimla's social swirl

In creating the enigma that was Shimla, there were some vital social ingredients with amusing labels. There were the 'grass-widows': young married women who spent a season on their own, while their husbands sweltered it out in the districts. Then there were members of the 'fishing fleet' – again young women, but unmarried. They sailed out every year from Britain in search of husbands; and the unsuccessful ones who sailed back without a wedding band or even an engagement ring, were termed 'returned empties'. The male counterpoise came from a number of young officials and army officers. Once *kala jagahs*, or dark nooks at parties arrived (where a couple could sit out the evening without an eyebrow being raised), Victorian morality stewing in the heat of the plains, screamed much louder. Even in England, Shimla was a place to be spoken of with bated breath while the minions of the Raj kept at bay from the inner circle, and began bestowing the town with sobriquets like 'Mount Olympus' and 'Home of the Little Tin Gods'.

As Rudyard Kipling put it:

Jack Barrett went to Quetta
Because they told him to.
He left his wife at Simla
On three-fourths his monthly screw:
Jack Barrett died at Quetta
Ere the next month's pay he drew.

Jack Barrett went to Quetta
He didn't understand
The reason of his transfer
From the pleasant mountain-land:
The season was September,
And it killed him out of hand

Jack Barrett went to Quetta
And there gave up the ghost
Attempting two men's duty
In that very healthy post;
And Mrs. Barrett mourned for him
Five lively months at most.

80

WALK SIX

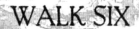

The Two Jakho Walks

Jakho (Jakhoo, Jakhu) is the hill that dominates
Shimla and is topped by the temple to Bhagwan
Hanuman. These are two walks; the first circles the hill
and the other climbs it. They can be combined to
become a single longer one.

The Jakho Round
From the Ridge and back circling the hill.

 DIRECTION, APPROXIMATE TIME AND DISTANCE

This walk does not go up to the famous Hanuman temple atop the hill but only circles the hill and covers about six kilometres. Plan for two hours or more. (The next walk described here, 'Shimla's Highest' is to the top of Jakho.)

 SUGGESTED TIME OF THE DAY

The ideal time to begin this walk would be in the morning or latest by afternoon.

★ **HIGHLIGHTS**

Views and flora
Built heritage
Lakkar Bazaar

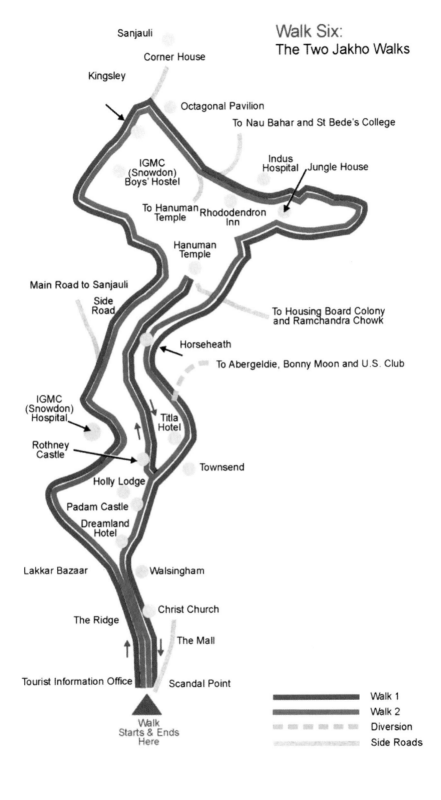

Walk Six:
The Two Jakho Walks

Sanjauli

Corner House

Kingsley

Octagonal Pavilion

To Nau Bahar and St Bede's College

Indus
Hospital   Jungle House

IGMC
(Snowdon)
Boys' Hostel

To Hanuman
Temple   Rhododendron
Inn

Hanuman
Temple

Main Road to Sanjauli

Side
Road

To Housing Board Colony
and Ramchandra Chowk

Horseheath

To Abergeldie, Bonny Moon and U.S. Club

IGMC
(Snowdon)
Hospital

Titla
Hotel

Rothney
Castle

Townsend

Holly Lodge

Padam Castle

Dreamland
Hotel

Lakkar Bazaar

Walsingham

Christ Church

The Ridge

The Mall

Tourist Information Office

Scandal Point

Walk
Starts & Ends
Here

Walk 1

Walk 2

Diversion

Side Roads

A walk to court by

The 'Jakho Round' as it was popularly known, was a standard walk or courting move on foot, horseback or by rickshaw. The route described in this walk has been modified from the original one to minimise the parts where there is excessive traffic or population and runs roughly parallel to and above the older one. A section of this walk is what used to be along the old Five Benches Road.

In an episode from the epic *Ramayana*, when Bhagwan Rama's younger bother, Lakshman (Laxman) lay mortally wounded on a battlefield in Lanka, Bhagwan Hanuman went in search of the legendary *sanjivini* herb which was required to cure him. Legend has it that during his search, he made a stopover at Jakho, the hill that towers over Shimla. A variation of the story declares that one of his sandals fell here.

The Ridge, Lakkar Bazaar and Snowdon

Start from the Ridge and move towards the Lakkar Bazaar which is known for its wooden souvenirs and trinkets. The views from Lakkar Bazaar are impressive and a monsoon sunset could raise an eyebrow or two. The foreground includes the Bharari spur, Stirling Castle and the Elysium spur. As you go along, the snow-clad peaks of Greater Himalaya also become visible.

Cross the bazaar in the direction of the Indira Gandhi Medical College and Hospital (IGMC), formerly Snowdon, the residence of the British commander-in-chief of the Indian Army. All traces of the old building are gone. This used to be a large half-timbered structure which was extensively renovated when Lord Kitchener came to India as the Commander-in-Chief in 1902. The location still offers splendid views of the hills and snow ranges that lie past Shimla. Just short of the gates, the hillside has a couple of the few remaining holly trees of town.

The snow pits

Snowdon has one of the last surviving snow pits of Shimla. Many of the larger estates had these in one of their sunless corners. A pit, normally about twenty feet deep was dug and covered with a roof. All through the winter this would be packed with snow that under its own weight compacted into ice; and in the days before refrigeration, apart from the obvious uses of ice, this also served as a meat store.

Trees and tablets

Two hundred metres past the gates of Snowdon, near a newly built structure on your right, just above the road, there is a road that climbs up the hill to the right. A large board marks it to the Boys Hostel and Staff Residences.

Follow this road that zigzags on the initial stretch and has some interesting bits of flora. The trees with the deep green thick needle-like leaves are the Himalayan yew, *taxus baccata* and apart from their serene majesty, they also yield Taxol that is used in the treatment of cancer. The other trees here include rhododendrons and oak. Other foliage along this stretch consists of wild roses, geraniums, strawberries, begonias and several varieties of ivy, ferns and moss.

Forks lead to residences of the dental college and to the boy's medical hostel; continue the walk through the trees towards Sanjauli on what in winter, can be a fairly cold stretch as it faces north. The big pale-yellow buildings of the doctors lie above and you circle the hill passing a brick house of the Kingsley Estate. As you turn the hill, below lies Sanjauli and the walk continues along the somewhat level road. Here, the road forms a horseshoe bend and rows of prayer-flags mark the huts of the Tibetans who live here. One track goes down left to Corner House, the official residence of the municipal commissioner and the Sanjauli Bazaar. A landmark is a small octagonal pavilion with a tablet that reads that it was built in the memory of the 'Late Babu Nagar Mull Bajoria of No. 212 Cornwallis Street, Calcutta who breathed his last at Simla on 22-6-1933.'

This walk traces the horseshoe and turns right towards a road lined with cedar trees; the initial stretch leads to the Indus Hospital. The road below this has a constant traffic flow and was once called the "Ladies' Mile". While the newer residents would well be convinced that this is so named after the girls' college that lies at one end, in all likelihood the name came when the town's ladies began using it to practise their riding. And the high cliff that lay between this and the walk path was referred to as the 'Devil's Paintbox' because the rock-face was constantly changing colours with the seasons – their rain or sunshine.

A route option

If you have doubts about the location of the turnoff near Bothwell Lodge, then carry on this road that will go past the Government College for Boys to bustling Sanjauli. The site of this college was once known as North Stoneham and held the Asiatic Christian Orphanage that was established by Mrs Harriet Tytler in April 1869. The object was to provide education and industrial training to European and Eurasian orphaned girls. In 1904-05, the structure was rebuilt and opened by the Lieutenant Governor of the Punjab, Sir Charles Rivaz.

At Sanjauli Chowk, the crossroad, there is a narrow road on the right that rises sharply off the main road and leads to Corner House. Carry on past this in the direction of the Indus Hospital. This is the stretch described above as the road lined by cedar trees and is some fifty metres higher than the Ladies' Mile.

Just short of the Indus Hospital, the road has a fork turning down – that in turn divides into two more roads just further down. One leads to the Indus Hospital and the other goes down to the Nau Bahar Chowk. At the Nau Bahar crossroad, just above St. Bede's College, the road turning right was once called the Lovers' Lane as it fulfilled the need for seclusion and privacy that lovers sought. More popularly, it was called the Forest Hill Road. Forest Hill was one of the old houses on this road that has now been rebuilt to house the Radha Saomi Satsang. Yet another landmark is the crossroad outside its gate which is called Ramchandra Chowk after Mr Ramchandra, a distinguished civil servant who lived at Forest Hill. Short of Forest Hill, the road that goes down to the left leads to Raj Bhavan, the official residence of the state governor of Himachal Pradesh. If you have selected this route option, you can look up the section on this road in the walk titled the 'Heritage Miles'.

Above Indus Hospital and towards the Ridge

For this round it is suggested not to take this fork and turn right on a mildly rising slope. An incongruous sign in Hindi is hidden among the trees on the right marking the direction for the Jakho temple. This road carries on above the Indus Hospital. On the right is a small hotel, the Rhododendron Inn. This is a quieter and wooded track that opens pleasant views at different points.

Just above the large well-marked structure of the hospital, the road develops a sharper climb that leads to the microwave tower. En route the view has deep woods and the peak of Choor Chandni, the highest in the sub-Himalayan region is also visible.

The Choor Chandni

At over 3,600 metres the peak of Choor Chandni is the one that holds on to the snows for the longest and grabs them first along the sub-Himalayan belt. Some of this snow used to be sent packed into ice to the court of the Mughal kings of Delhi. There is an ancient temple of Chooreshwar Mahadev at its top dedicated to Shirgul, a devotee of Bhagwan Shiva. Over time and after many local legends, the characteristics of the devotee and Shiva have practically merged into one.

The name 'Choor Chandni' loosely translates as the 'mountain of the silver bangle'. For on moonlit nights, when the silvery light encircles its snowy slopes, shining silver bangles do appear to be jingling against the dark sky.

About a kilometre ahead, is an unmistakable crossroad that sends routes in various directions: on the right a road goes up to the temple of Bhagwan Hanuman on Jakho's top, on the left it goes past a newly built structure and down through the Housing Board's colony to arrive at Ramchandra Chowk. This was the place where five benches were once placed was hence named the 'Five Benches Road'. This walk route goes right along a steadily descending road. On the right above are a couple of Shimla's old houses, Horseheath being the first along the way. Walk up to the rather crumbly, but very pretty house with attractive woodwork called Titla Hotel that has elaborately corbelled and turned brackets and well wrought valances.

An alternative here is to plunge down on the left past several government houses, via the old squash courts, up to the gates of the old U.S. Club (United Services Club), which now houses the offices of the P.W.D. On this route lie two old houses, Abergeldie and Bonny Moon that also functioned as hotels in Shimla's early years.

This walk, however, is towards Holly Lodge along the level road that goes past Titla Hotel. Past Townsend on the left, this walk ends just below Holly Lodge.

The sharp plunge, a section of the main pedestrian road to the Hanuman temple atop Jakho, is taken now. This also displays a good view of the town and the snow peaks beyond. And during the monsoons, you can view some superb sunsets from here. This road will bring you to the Ridge near Christ Church. Should you choose, you can also climb up to the temple from this point or from the bifurcation mentioned earlier.

Shimla's Highest

From the Ridge to the Hanuman temple and then, circling the hill to return to the Ridge.

 DIRECTION, APPROXIMATE TIME AND DISTANCE

This goes up to the temple dedicated to Bhagwan Hanuman and then on above Sanjauli to circle the hill. Backtracking, this follows a section of the route described in 'The Jakho Round' and returns via Snowdon and Lakkar Bazaar to the Ridge. The total walk route covers a little over five kilometres. Plan for two hours or more.

 SUGGESTED TIME OF THE DAY

Again, the pleasure of this walk is best experienced in the morning or afternoon.

 **HIGHLIGHTS**

Rothney Castle
Jakho Temple
The views from Jakho

From the Ridge

At 2,455 metres, Jakho hill towers over Shimla. Replete with history and architectural charm, there are several houses along its steep 1.5 kilometre climb. This starts from the Ridge and lies sandwiched between the Children's Section of the State Library and Christ Church.

The forested hill of Jakho is crowned by a temple dedicated to Bhagwan Hanuman. Sunrises and sunsets witnessed from this vantage spot are spectacular enough to become a lifelong memory, especially during the monsoons.

Walsingham

Above Walsingham, the residence of Shimla's Deputy Commissioner, the road to Jakho turns right in front of the Dreamland Hotel. The name Walsingham may be inspired from the sacred site in North Norfolk in the U.K. The story of the site in Norfolk goes that a millennium ago, a widow, Richeldis de Faverches had a vision where the Virgin Mary appeared to her in the setting of a house in Nazareth. The widow was commanded to build the house whose dimensions were given. When workmen began work, they found the going hard. That night, the lady heard singing coming from the site. To her surprise she saw that the position had been shifted by a good two hundred feet, the building was complete and angels were departing. This became a place of pilgrimage in England and was visited by King Henry XIII. When Thomas Cromwell (1485-1540), carried out the dissolution of monasteries in England, Walsingham was burned to the ground. The poem 'The Wrecks of Walsingham' went,

Bitter, bitter, O to behold
The grass to grow
Where the walls of Walsingham
So stately did show.

Centuries later, the shrine was rebuilt and the first modern-day pilgrimage to Walsingham was in 1897.

It may also be conjectured that Shimla's Walsingham, built in *dhajji*, owes its name to Sir Francis Walsingham (1530-1590), who rose to become the Secretary of State under Queen Elizabeth I. This made him one of the most powerful men of his time and he served as a protector of both Crown and Realm. In Shimla's context, the role of the deputy commissioner under the colonial government was not dissimilar.

Holly Lodge and Rothney Castle

Two of Shimla's finest houses lie on the slope up to Jakho and are neighbours. The first on the way up is Holly Lodge that in the 1830s was one of the early houses to be built in Shimla. At the instance of Sophia Anne Cotton, wife of G.E.L. Cotton, Bishop of Calcutta and Metropolitan of India, a Girls School was established here in 1866, till it moved to its present premises at Auckland House in 1868. Later, a well known resident was Lieutenant-General Sir Gerald De Courcy Morton, who died at Curragh, Ireland in 1906; a memorial tablet to him was erected at Shimla's Christ Church and may still be seen. This then passed into the hands Raja Sir Padam Singh of Bushehr (Bushair) who was one of the leading Hill Chiefs; the property is still with his descendants. The present occupant is Raja Virbhadra Singh who was elected the Chief Minister of Himachal Pradesh in 1983.

Just above is Rothney Castle which was built by a Colonel Rothney in 1838 and then known as Rothney House. In 1843, the house passed into the hands of a Dr Carte who established the Simla Bank Corporation, which later shifted to the site of the Grand Hotel. This then became the property of a Mr A.H. Mathews and he was followed by Mr P. Mitchell, from whom it was purchased by its most famous owner, Mr A.O. Hume, founder of the Indian National Congress – the organisation that went on spearhead India's Freedom Movement. By now, the word 'House' had also been substituted for 'Castle' and Hume set out to establish the Castle's character by totally overhauling the premises to make this one of Shimla's most magnificent homes. Glass was used extensively and the locals still refer to it as *'sheesha wali kothi'* or the house of glass.

Hume's extensive ornithological collection was also housed here till he donated it to the British Museum. After a few other owners, including the consuls-general of Germany, Rothney Castle passed into the hands of Lala Chunna Mull of Delhi in the first quarter of the twentieth century, and remains with his descendants.

A little word of caution – this area has several monkeys and is the stronghold of the town's famous macaques. Do not act threatening, or look them in the eye or carry visible foodstuffs. The other things they seem tempted to examine are glasses and purses with shiny clasps.

Jakho Temple

After Rothney Castle, the climb holds its sharp angle right up to the temple, which is a dressed stone structure dedicated to Bhagwan Hanuman. There are no restrictions on non-Hindus entering the temple, but shoes must be removed outside. For a token amount, one of the souvenir sellers outside will keep an eye on them.

In season, hundreds of visitors and devotees climb the slope or take the tortuous drive from the direction of Sanjauli. The temple is built on a raised platform and is surrounded by open spaces.

The views from Jakho

The town flows out of Jakho's slopes and the view from the top has all the magnificence one would expect from this vantage point. From west to east (left to right facing the snows), some of the major peaks and ranges are as follows.

The Dhauladhar range is a southern branch of the main Himalayan chain. These mountains are at their most majestic in Himachal's districts of Mandi, Kangra and Chamba. The highest peak of this range is the Dhauladhar (5,639 m) or 'white mountain' that stands behind Dharamsala, the district headquarters of Kangra. As many of the Himalayan ranges run parallel to one another, these pop up at other points too. Adjoining the Dhauladhar, are the Pir Panjal Mountains that are a part of the Middle Himalaya and flow out of Jammu and Kashmir to enter the district of Chamba in Himachal Pradesh. The Pir Panjal move in a southeasterly direction with an average elevation of 4,000 m.

Then comes the Manimahesh Kailash (5,655 m) and this is one of the many peaks held sacred to Bhagwan Shiva in the Himalaya. It rises near Chamba above the Manimahesh Lake and the Chobu Pass. Moving right, Kamru Nag Dhar is a series of high hills with woods and are around the secluded temple of Kamru Nag (3,082 m). Held in considerable veneration, the deity

Kamru Nag's anger is regarded to cause unwanted rain and floods. The primary offering to the *deuta* is of ornaments and coins that are cast in the lake that lies by the temple. The hill of Shikari Devi (3,359 m) is also in this direction and its windswept top is crowned by a roofless temple dedicated to the goddess with the same name.

Gepang Goh (5,870 m) is in Trans Himalayan Lahaul and lies close to the town of Keylong. This has a group of summits and is held sacred to Lahaul's patron deity Gepang (Gyephang, Gyepang).

Standing side by side, the Deo Tibba (6,000 m) and Indrasan (6,220 m) are prominent peaks in the Kullu region. Mahun Nag (2,233 m) is a part of the Middle Himalaya and is a hill held sacred to the deity Mahun Nag, interpreted by some as Karna of the epic *Mahabharata*. Then the Great Himalayan Range becomes visible and has heights that cross 6,500 m. These mountains divide the Lower Himalaya and the cold deserts of the Trans Himalaya.

Choti (Little) Shali (2,588 m) is a distinctive hill in the Lesser Himalaya whose treeless face is towards Shimla; this has the rain-fed lake of Kariali on its northern face. Gushu Pishu (5,583 m) can be seen between the Choti Shali and the higher Shali peak. These twin peaks with a height variation of a few metres are located in the district of Kinnaur.

Shali (2,822 m) is the highest hill in Shimla's immediate vicinity and while its southern face is characteristically bare, the northern one is thickly wooded. A hike trail leads to the top which is crowned by a small temple dedicated to the goddess Bhimakali. Raldang (5,500 m) lies in the district of Kinnaur and many believe that spirits of the dead people of Kinnaur go there to reside and from its heights bless the land.

The peak of Kufri (2,670 m, also called the Mahasu peak), takes the eastern edge of the view from Jakho.

The way back

From the temple, you can backtrack or take the road that leads to Sanjauli and is used by vehicles to reach this point. With your back to the gates of the temple, turn left for this walk. The road zigzags initially and at the end of the squiggles, turn left again. By and large, this is a steady downhill walk shaded by trees of cedar, oak and rhododendron. About a kilometre and a half down, just above the Sanjauli Bazaar, there is a horseshoe bend marked by a pavilion and scores of Buddhist prayer flags. Without stepping down towards the bazaar, continue along the bend and the road it feeds. This moves just below the Doctors' Residences and soon zigzags down to the main road that connects Sanjauli to IGMC. The road now carries on past the gates of the IGMC to Lakkar Bazaar and the Ridge.

This leg is along a portion of the walk described just before this one.

The story of Baba Mast Ram

In his capacity as Shimla's very own bard, Rudyard Kipling was moved enough to pen a poem on the 'artful *bandar*' calling him a 'gleesome fleasome thou'. Jakho still remains Shimla's simian stronghold and connected with these rhesus macaques is the story of Charles de Russet.

The son of a French architect and contractor, Russet was a pupil at the local Bishop Cotton School. Sometime in the 1880s he left his studies, renounced Christianity and joined the fakir at Jakho temple. For two years he underwent the severe rigours of a novice. He lived under a tree and the attendant who brought him food was his only human contact. He made over the property he had inherited to his sisters and was uncommunicative about his reasons for abandoning his former religion.

John C. Oman, a professor of natural science met him in 1894 and recorded: '. . . he was particularly well clothed, though not in any *sadhu* style I have ever seen. He informed me that he lived his solitary life in the neighbourhood of Simla throughout the year, even in winter when the snow lay deep upon the mountains.'

In time Russet was accepted into the priesthood and became a venerated figure. For a long time he was attached to the Jakho temple and was known as Baba Mast Ram. Then, according to one source, Russet left Shimla with a band of *sadhus* and was never heard of again. Another declared that he began living in seclusion at a temple some distance from Shimla where he 'avoided recognition, shunned Europeans and seemed to have forgotten his mother tongue.'

Russet is also regarded to have had the ability to communicate with monkeys. A story is told of Raja Sir Daljit Singh of Kapurthala who, disgusted with their destructiveness, got Russet to 'tell them' to keep away from his house, Strawberry Hill in Chotta Shimla. It is said that even now monkeys do not enter the grounds.

Banksia roses in bloom. ▲

▲ Khaleej Pheasant.

Monal Pheasant. ▶

▲ *Observatory Hill that holds Viceregal Lodge – view from Prospect Hill.*

(facing page): Cedars under snow. ▶

Manorville, the former residence of Rajkumari Amrit Kaur. ▼

◀ Christ Church at night.

Interior of Christ
Church. ▼

A doorway and sundial at Christ Church Lodge.

The Clarke's Hotel. ▼

▼ *Woodville, a stately art deco mansion.*

Kali Bari temple.

Jakho temple. ▶

*The temple near
Annandale.* ▼

Temple on the links at Naldehra. ▲

▼ *Ponies near Mashobra.*

A snow walk in Naldehra.

The cedar forest of Shimla's water catchment area, near Charabra.

WALK SEVEN

Down Southern Slopes

Down to the temple of a local harvest deity,
Dhanu Devta.

This unusual walk is down Shimla's southern valley to a place called Bihargaon – while this is the general term used for the area, there are smaller villages with individual names.

The walk goes past one of the old graveyards to touch the three temples of Dhanu Devta and then climbs back to town via pine-draped Tuttikandi, or through Khalini.* It is all downhill while going and uphill on the return. A fair test for both lungs and legs, the round trip from the level of the Mall covers six to eight kilometres. Plan for four hours or more.

SUGGESTED TIME OF THE DAY

This walk is best done is the morning.

★ HIGHLIGHTS

The old graveyard
The woods
The temples of Dhanu Devta
The villages of Kalyana, Klare and Kaloa
Tuttikandi

---

* This area is witnessing a fair bit of construction of roads and buildings and what was valid at the time of writing may have altered down the line.

Walk Seven:
Down Southern Slopes

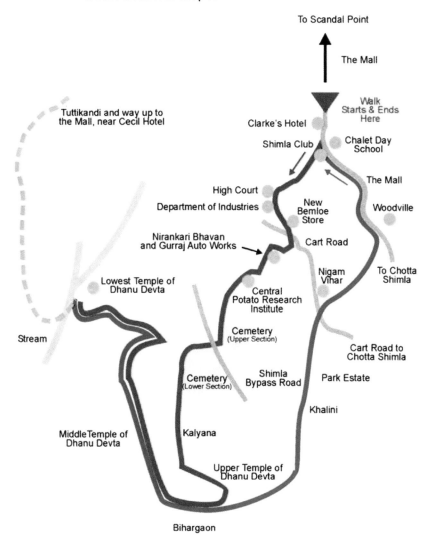

To Scandal Point

The Mall

Walk Starts & Ends Here

Tuttikandi and way up to the Mall, near Cecil Hotel

Clarke's Hotel

Shimla Club

Chalet Day School

The Mall

High Court

Department of Industries

New Bemloe Store

Woodville

Nirankari Bhavan and Gurraj Auto Works

Cart Road

Lowest Temple of Dhanu Devta

Nigam Vihar

To Chotta Shimla

Central Potato Research Institute

Stream

Cemetery (Upper Section)

Cart Road to Chotta Shimla

Cemetery (Lower Section)

Shimla Bypass Road

Park Estate

Khalini

Middle Temple of Dhanu Devta

Kalyana

Upper Temple of Dhanu Devta

Bihargaon

The Way Out
The Way Back
Diversion
Side Roads

The old graveyard

The starting point of this walk is the slope that leads off the Mall near the High Court of Himachal Pradesh down to the level of the Cart Road (Circular Road) via the office of the Department of Industries. Both the High Court and the Industries Department have large new buildings and are quite unmistakable. This pocket also has several old and attractive houses which are the Bemloe Cottages occupied by government officials and army officers. Once you are at the level of the Cart Road (today's Circular Road that carries vehicular traffic), move left towards the New Bemloe Store. Opposite the store another sharp slope heads down towards the Potato Research Institute. Carry on past the gates of the Institute on this downhill stretch.

This road arrives at the Shimla bypass and faces the gates of the cemetery – a section of this cemetery also lies above the road. Burials in this cemetery commenced in 1850, though it was formally consecrated in 1857. The original site was extended in 1871 and the cemetery was in use till the first quarter of the twentieth century. (The Sanjauli cemetery was used after this.) Several of Shimla's early builders and prominent citizens were interred in this peaceful grove – including H.S. Harington, builder of the Kalka-Shimla Railway and several army and civil officers.

The temples

On the bypass, just above the cemetery and by a couple of small shops, there is a narrow metalled road that branches down to the right. (There is also one on the left that goes to the locality of Kanlog.) This walk goes past some of the Potato Research Institute's residential quarters and other buildings. Carry on to the village of Kalyana, where you turn right and head straight down to a fairly recently built temple of Devi Durga. The road now turns to a narrow path and immediately below the temple, turn right and continue down.

On the left comes a large brightly painted house and past this on the next spur you can see the red roof of the highest temple of Dhanu Devta. This roof acts like a beacon. Walk towards this through what are still open fields. There are a couple of little gullies here, the first has walnut trees shading it and the next has a little stream, and then begin the thick woods of deodar. Through a fairly well defined path that now meets with a vehicular road on the make, this walk takes you to the middle temple of Dhanu Devta that is a short wooden tower. The track partially follows an age-old kuhl, a water channel that goes from its primary source to one village and then another – with each maintaining its own

section as it were. From this village, called Klare (a part of the Bihargaon area) turn right through the fields that depending on the time of year will have wheat, maize or vegetables. This path will take you to the lowest temple of Dhanu Devta that is perhaps the prettiest one, especially given its setting in a small glade, under tall cedars and with the town of

Shimla high up at the head of the slope. This glade makes for a good picnic spot.

The way back

From this point, you can cross the stream and climb through the spur of Tuttikandi which is covered with pine trees. The melange of paths and the absence of a definitive landmark here, make this a difficult route to define. But broadly, head upward and a take loose turn along the protruding spur in the direction of Shimla. A narrow path arrives at the base of what used to be the Tuttikandi zoo. Cross this, then cross the bypass, keep climbing steadily up and you will reach the Circular Road just below the Cecil.

Alternatively, backtrack from the valley and climb back through the village of Klare in the direction of the village of Kaloa. This is the highest village of Bihargaon and from here, climb on through the wide fields. You will reach dense pockets of age-old habitation that are experiencing abrasion due to the expansion of urbanisation in this region. This path, now a road, leads on to the residential colony of the forest department and then on to Khalini from where you can take a bus back into town, or continue the walk through the Park Estate, by Nigam Vihar and then up to the level of the Mall.

WALK EIGHT

The Northern Tracks

To the Bharari spur.

A relatively unexplored area full of good walks along wide roads or narrow paths is the Bharari spur. There are no grand monuments of built heritage along this track, but there are some attractive old cottages, patches of woodland and some superb views.

 SUGGESTED TIME OF THE DAY

Take this walk in the morning or afternoon.

★ **HIGHLIGHTS**

The views
The paths
Built heritage (mostly cottages) and the former Elysium, Longwood and Craig Dhu hotels.

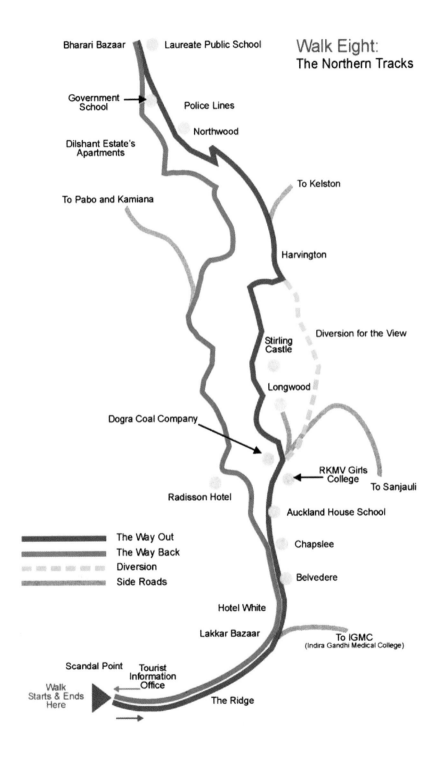

Walk Eight:
The Northern Tracks

Bharari Bazaar

Laureate Public School

Government School

Police Lines

Northwood

Dilshant Estate's Apartments

To Pabo and Kamiana

To Kelston

Harvington

Diversion for the View

Stirling Castle

Longwood

Dogra Coal Company

RKMV Girls College

To Sanjauli

Radisson Hotel

Auckland House School

Chapslee

The Way Out
The Way Back
Diversion
Side Roads

Belvedere

Hotel White

Lakkar Bazaar

To IGMC
(Indira Gandhi Medical College)

Scandal Point

Tourist Information Office

Walk Starts & Ends Here

The Ridge

Down to Auckland House School and Chapslee

Start from the Ridge, step down from the Lakkar Bazaar towards Auckland House School and reach the Longwood rise. At the base of the slope lies Auckland House's junior school in a house called Belvedere – this was where Dr Menkel of the Seventh Day Adventists ran his spa for several years till he shifted it to the Chaura Maidan area in the 1940s and where it still stands. Auckland House was the position where the Governor General of India, Lord Auckland (1835-1842) had his residence. Adjoining this and just short of the school is Chapslee which acts as a select hotel and is perhaps the only residence in town that is preserved in a time-lock that belongs to a century now past.

Gobelin tapestries, delft tiled fireplaces, Murano chandeliers and drapes from the Doge's palace in Venice still evoke a long gone way of life. On 1 October 1838 the fateful Simlah Manifesto that launched the disastrous First Afghan War was issued from its rooms. In 1848, the house was purchased by General Peter Innes of the Bengal Army who gave it the name, Chapslee. After 1870,

this repeatedly changed hands and one resident was Sir Courtney Ilbert, after whom the famous Ilbert Bill that proposed to allow Indian judges to try Europeans was named. In 1896, Chapslee became the property of Sir Arthur Milford Ker of the Alliance Bank of Simla who practically rebuilt this to create one of the finest residences in town. Exactly a century after the fateful Manifesto was issued, in 1938, this was purchased by Raja Charanjit Singh of Kapurthala (d. 1970) as a summer residence and Chapslee is still with his descendants.

After the school lies the present-day Rashtriya Kanya Maha Vidyalaya (the Government College for Girls). This held the erstwhile Elysium Hotel – and the town's old residents still refer to this promontory as the Elysium Spur. Interestingly, the name 'Elysium', the 'blessed fields' in Greek mythology, was given to this area as a compliment to Lord Auckland's sisters, Fanny and Emily Eden who had accompanied their brother to India.

In 1947, when the bloodbath of the partition and the creation of India and Pakistan took place, the Elysium Hotel belonged to Messrs Hussain Bux and Co. They had a tailoring establishment at Scandal Point and this was converted into a protected camp for Muslims.

The hundred metres between the gates of Auckland House and the edge of the Longwood spur are along the highway, where in all likelihood you will be either clawing the hill or clutching the railing and damning the invention of the automobile horn – if not the automobile itself.* Where the highway ends, there is practically a mélange of roads and paths that move off the curve of this hairpin bend.

---

* At the time of writing, the process of redoing an old tunnel in the area has started and is likely to ease the traffic congestion here.

Craig Dhu Hotel

At the 'Longwood' hairpin bend on the left there is a small shop, the Dogra Coal Company and an STD booth. Adjoining this is a road, largely shaded by oaks, which takes a short dip down and then a mild slope up and finally levels out for a major portion of this walk. About a hundred metres from the fork is a rather deceptive turn down to the left; do not take this. On the main route are several old cottages of *dhajji*, brick and stone that evoke Shimla's heyday.

A short diversion at the hairpin bend can also take you the former Longwood Hotel, where one of Rudyard Kipling's famous characters, the indomitable Mrs Hauksbee lived.

About two hundred metres along the walk route, the large wooden structure on the right was once the Craig Dhu Hotel that served as a residence for many small families and for officers posted to Shimla on temporary duty.

By Harvington whose rooms briefly served as the High Court of the Punjab, and just short of the recently built Judges Residences, the road sets one branch off to Kelston and the Bharari Bazaar to the left, while the right turn brings you back to the highway. Here, in the dip is a large concrete water-tank which used to have one of Shimla ice-pits. This pit was about twenty feet deep and covered with a roof. Here, snow was shovelled in through the winter and by its own weight, this would compact itself into ice. In the years before refrigeration, ice pits like this one were used for both cooling drinks and preserving meats.

You could take a little stroll on this stretch that has excellent views of the northern snow-covered ranges.

Downhill to Bharari and back

With the big water tank on your left, head downhill. Continue past the retaining walls of Harvington, to the start of the slope that leads up to the Kelston housing colony. The road to Kelston branches off to the right. At this point, two roads lead to the Bharari Bazaar. One is the sharp plunge adjoining the rain shelter and the other is milder slope which forms the centre road. This is all downhill and largely through woods of Himalayan oak.

Northwood, which is the next structure on the track, is an attractive dressed stone house which lies partly screened from the road. Immediately below this are the Police Lines. The Lines once held the residence of the Maharaja of Bharatpur and the wide field was filled by water and formed a shallow lake. Do take a moment to examine the somewhat crumbly house that lies by the gate of the field and houses police offices. For all its seediness, this has noteworthy aesthetic forms in its stonework.

Continue the downhill walk up to the Laureate Public School. The Bharari Bazaar lies just past this. This walk does not enter the bazaar and takes the level road that lies to the left as you descend and is practically at a level. (The couple of small tea shops in the bazaar do offer the option of a brief stopover.) This road lies just below the Government School, goes past the local bus stop, moves on for about two kilometres till it reaches the Lakkar Bazaar again. It goes past the Radisson Hotel at Goodwood to finally climb up to the Lakkar Bazaar again. Parts of this walk are through a protected forest of oak and rhododendron.

Extensions

From Bharari you can walk to the villages that lie to right of the Seismic Recording Centre, or to the villages of Pabo and Kamiana. Longer treks can be made to Kiar Koti and Tattapani. A guide is suggested for these.

WALK NINE

The Bazaar Walk

A short walk through Shimla's Lower Bazaar.

DIRECTION, APPROXIMATE TIME AND DISTANCE

The Lower Bazaar runs roughly parallel to the Mall. This walk starts at the D.C.'s office and winds up at the Sher-e-Punjab end. Depending on the time you take to dissect the shops, sample the wares, jostle and be jostled, the walking time is just about half an hour. The distance is barely a kilometre and a half.

 SUGGESTED TIME OF THE DAY

You can take this walk at any time of the day.

★ **HIGHLIGHTS**

The architecture
The shops
The Ganj
The tunnel

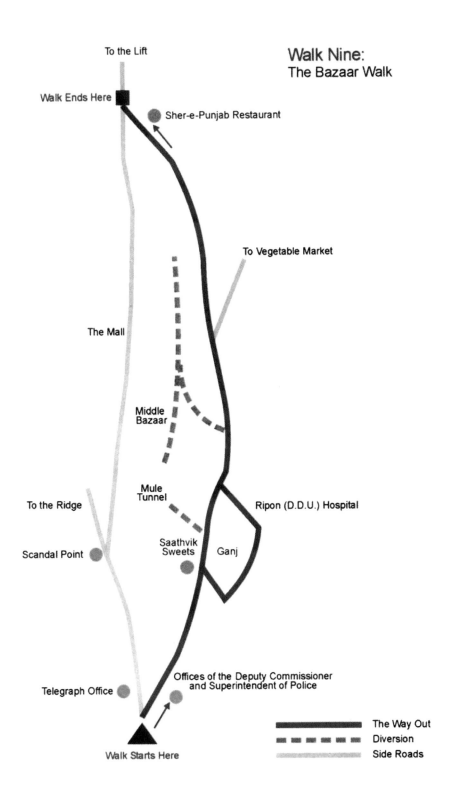

To the Lift

Walk Ends Here

Sher-e-Punjab Restaurant

Walk Nine:
The Bazaar Walk

To Vegetable Market

The Mall

Middle
Bazaar

Mule
Tunnel

To the Ridge

Ripon (D.D.U.) Hospital

Scandal Point

Saathvik
Sweets

Ganj

Offices of the Deputy Commissioner
and Superintendent of Police

Telegraph Office

The Way Out

Diversion

Side Roads

Walk Starts Here

Lower Bazaar

This is a thickly populated area that over a hundred and twenty years ago was described by Rudyard Kipling in *Kim* as: 'The crowded rabbit-warren that climbs up from the valley to the Town Hall at an angle of forty-five. A man who knows his way there can defy all the police of India's summer capital. So cunningly does verandah communicate with verandah, alley-way with alley-way, and bolt-hole with bolt hole.' The description still holds true – the Lower Bazaar is connected to the Mall by steep staircases and twisting alleys. Incidentally, Shimla's southern slope, of which the Lower Bazaar is a major component, is regarded as one of the most densely populated hill slopes in the world (the others belong to the Andes). A major determinant of the town's character and social ethos is this market place, which remains a reflection of the Indian market-centric social ethos.

Like the Mall, the Lower Bazaar has both commercial establishments and residences and this keeps the area vibrant even after shop hours. Giving physical expression to the phrase

'cheek by jowl', this street is packed with a variety of colours, scents and sounds. This mass of people is also a distillation of Shimla's social spectrum where designer jeans go hand in hand with the *reshta*, the traditional loose fitting tunic worn by women in these hills.

The walk begins from the deputy commissioner's office, which lies just below the Telegraph Office on the Mall. The walk loops gently down and then gradually climbs back to the level of the Mall. The bazaar has some good examples of indigenous architecture and the most unexpected places will reveal intricate carvings on eaves boards, lintels and columns – some of the older houses even have cotton wool stuffed behind walls, which acts like extra-effective double glazing.

The bazaar has several eating-places, *halwais* that sell Indian sweets, vendors of assorted wares and jewellers.

Opposite a sweetshop called Saatvik Sweets, is the turn off

for the Ganj. This lies just below the bazaar and is a wholesale market that was established by the British Political Agent to the Hill States, Sir Herbert Edwardes in the mid-nineteenth century. While you take the second turn to the Ganj, the building on the left loosely imitates the former Railway Booking Office on the Mall. If the one on the Mall has a flatter, more 'English' dome,

Architectural detail from the Middle Bazaar

this one is quite Saracenic. There is a large temple dedicated to Bhagwan Krishna in the Ganj. These clusters of shops sell rice and pulses and some even have small flour mills rumbling in little back rooms. With all their vibrant colours and bags of chillies and beans these rows seem to resemble an artist's palette. A light breeze may carry with it whiffs of coriander and cumin and of so many of the spices and condiments used in Indian cuisine.

Ripon Hospital and then back

While one would hardly recommend a place packed with patients and doctors as a 'tourist site', the Ripon Hospital (now called the Deen Dayal Upadhyaya Hospital) may well be one of the largest structures in India to still survive with Swiss Bavarian architectural forms. This lies just below the Ganj and some of its gables are clearly visible. Its foundation stone was set by the Marquis of Ripon in 1882 and the hospital was opened for patients – both

European and Indian – on 14 May 1885 by Lord Dufferin. The architectural plan was prepared by Henry Irwin, who designed the façade as a large alpine villa. This site had originally held two houses, The Briars and Glen Cottage that had burned down in 1881. The initiative for establishing this hospital was taken by A.O. Hume and Sir Benjamin Franklin and the year that the hospital was opened, was also the year that Hume founded the Indian National Congress. The funds for this institution were almost wholly collected through donations and the original plaque on the hospital acknowledges all those who had a hand in its creation.

Returning to the level of the Ganj, you can take the slope back to the bazaar and go past the shed where once mules and other beasts of burden were tethered. On the other hand, you can backtrack and take a staircase up to the bazaar that goes past what a wag called 'the wholesale barber shop in the wholesale market.'

At the level of the bazaar is what is still called the Mule Tunnel. Through this, mule trains would carry a variety of goods (rice, flour or kerosene) to the interior.

Sections of the Lower Bazaar have the vegetable, meat and fish markets. The site of the meat market is believed to stand where the old Assembly Rooms once were – and where social gathering and even plays were staged in the early nineteenth century.

The bazaar meets the Mall towards the eastern end, about a hundred metres short of the Lift, near a *dhaba* (street side food-place) called the Sher-e-Punjab.

WALK TEN

A Suburban Walk

From the village of Charabra, which is en route to
Kufri, on the National Highway down to the
golf course at Naldehra.

DIRECTION, APPROXIMATE TIME AND DISTANCE

From Charabra, the walk goes down along narrow roads to Naldehra and is a relatively long one. There are three points where you can terminate the walk and return to Shimla. The first is Mashobra (three kilometres from Charabra), Baldian (six kilometres from Charabra) and Naldehra (ten kilometres from Charabra). At any of these points you can take a bus or taxi or have your car meet you to return to Shimla. Throughout the day, buses are available easily, though at times these are quite full and may rattle a bone or two.

Most of the walk between Charabra and Naldehra is downhill, barring a mild incline between Mashobra and the Fruit Research Station. Of course, you can walk back from Naldehra; and if you plan to do this, an early start is suggested. Then the return need not take you back to Charabra, but follow the highway to Shimla via Mashobra, Dhalli and Sanjauli.

 SUGGESTED TIME OF THE DAY

Considering the length of this walk, you should start in the morning or by early afternoon.

★ HIGHLIGHTS

Colonial cottages
The President's Retreat
The views
The woods and flora
Mashobra
Horticulture Research Station
Naldehra
Glade of Sipur, as an option

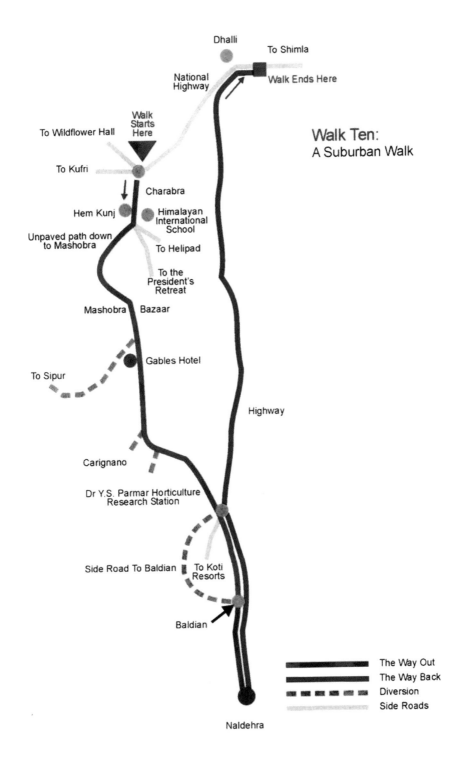

Dhalli

To Shimla

National
Highway

Walk Ends Here

Walk
Starts
Here

To Wildflower Hall

Walk Ten:
A Suburban Walk

To Kufri

Charabra

Hem Kunj

Himalayan
International
School

Unpaved path down
to Mashobra

To Helipad

To the
President's
Retreat

Mashobra   Bazaar

Gables Hotel

To Sipur

Highway

Carignano

Dr Y.S. Parmar Horticulture
Research Station

Side Road To Baldian

To Koti
Resorts

Baldian

The Way Out

The Way Back

Diversion

Side Roads

Naldehra

Charabra

Drive, take a taxi or bus to reach Charabra. The drive takes around forty minutes from the bus stand located by the Ice Skating Rink. If you prefer walking to the spot, the route is along the highway past Sanjauli and Dhalli; from the Mall the distance is approximately twelve kilometres.

At Charabra, short of the gates of the Hotel Wildflower Hall, turn left from the highway towards the President's Retreat. Through an area once called Mahasu, and through the village, that has a dozen or so small restaurants, the walk skirts old colonial houses which were built by those who preferred the quiet of these suburbs to the hectic social swirl of Shimla. Largely built of lath and plaster, in the *dhajji* style, many of these structures retain a considerable measure of their original character. The road is narrow and shaded by deodar trees. The views around are spectacular, which is perhaps one reason why the area was first built; there is the deep dip of the Mashobra valley, the Choti Shali and Shali and then the long line of snow-clad peaks.

Old Mahasu was perhaps the only part of India to initially have a tract, and then an administrative district named not after a specific place or town, but after a deity. There are a group of deities who are regarded to protect the area and have collectively been given the singular title 'Mahasu'. As Shimla grew and developed as the summer capital of British India, there were many who did not care for the town and opted for the suburbs. The area has had distinguished residents by the score and includes practically all the governor generals and viceroys of India who occupied the Retreat at various points. The Viceroy's Retreat is now with the President of India, and is visited by him for short periods. In 1972, at the time of signing the historical Simla

• A SUBURBAN WALK

Agreement with Pakistan, the former Prime Minister of India, Mrs Indira Gandhi stayed here.

In a house once called Dane's Folly, that has been rebuilt and is now called Hem Kunj, the governor of the state of Punjab also has his Retreat. And there hangs a tale. It is said that the house was built with the presumption that the town of Shimla would grow in these woods, and when that did not happen, its mournful owner gave it the name. More likely, the name came as a result of possessing the architectural characteristics of a folly.

Through the woods

Walk past Hem Kunj till you arrive at the gates of the Himalayan Public School, which will be on your left. The metalled road continues to the Kalyani helipad and to the President's Retreat. There is a way down to Mashobra that goes by the Retreat too, but expectedly, the entry to this area is restricted.

On the right, opposite the school gates, is the office of Hem Kunj's estate manager and some garages. A path adjoining these

goes down to the right and its steady descent is through patches of grassland speckled with broom, wild roses and daises; through woods of oak, cedar, spruce and holly enlivened with bushes of barberry and mistletoe, as well as with ferns, maidenhair and mosses. The bare soil is carpeted with oak leaves and apart from the scrunch of your feet over them, you may well hear a Himalayan thrush or the distant kettledrums of a *devta's* procession or even some rap music from a campsite down in the valley. The mid-distance has a view of the Shali peak and past this lie the snow clad ranges of the Greater Himalaya. About halfway down to Mashobra, on the right is a small orchard that is a part of the Presidential estate. This walk between Charabra and Mashobra Bazaar will take around forty minutes.

Mashobra Bazaar

The bazaar slowly starts climbing towards the estate of the former Maharaja of Faridkot. Past these impressive houses that can be but glimpsed from the road, a little to a side lies Carignano, which was first built by the Chevalier Fredrico Peliti, the Viceroy Lord Lytton's chef. Peliti named the place after his native village in Italy. A brilliant confectioner, he started the famous Peliti's Restaurant in Shimla which was alluded to in Rudyard Kipling's writings. Carignano was taken over by the U.S. Club as a suburban getaway for its members who utilised it for shooting expeditions too. A fire took the old building which was replaced by a small brick and wood structure. The estate wound its way into the hands of Shimla's Municipal Corporation and large water tanks that hold a substantial quantity of water bound for Shimla are located under the garden of Carignano. (If you would like to opt out of Charabra,

123

you can also start the walk from Mashobra, which is about twelve kilometres from the Mall.)

Hillock's Head

Continue on the mild climb towards the Horticulture Research Station (better known locally as the 'Fruit' Research Station). En route, the views still encompass the Shali peak (2,822 m), a tall largely bare hill that is the highest in the area. Past this are the snow covered ranges of the Greater Himalaya and the spread of peaks visible from various points. These span hundreds of kilometres: starting from the Dhauladhars in the west, to the Garhwal ranges in the east. In between they hold the mountains of Kullu and Kinnaur.

Now named after Dr Y.S. Parmar, the first Chief Minister of Himachal Pradesh, the Horticulture Research Station was called Hillock's Head and once belonged to Alexander Coutts, a viceregal tailor. Coutts introduced the English varieties of apple here; though India's Johnny Appleseed, Samuel Stokes later brought the American varieties that substantially transformed the economy of several pockets of these hills.

Designated as a Regional Horticulture Research Centre by the Indian Council of Agricultural Research in 1953, the centre conducts research on the high density planting of temperate fruits (apples, pews, cherries) and the control of pests with lower quantities of pesticides.

Down to Baldian

About a hundred metres short of the gates of the Fruit Research Station, when you are facing them, a road drops down to the left. Return from Coutts' garden and take this. This road steadily descends to the highway bound for Naldehra. At the end of the descent, there is a knot of paths and roads again and on your left lies the highway. Almost in front is a narrow road that climbs to the Koti Resort and on the right, there is a narrow track that moves downhill through the pines and cedars. While you may follow the highway to the village of Baldian, it is this last path that is suggested; this also winds its way to Baldian and is traffic free.

From Baldian's cluster of shops, the walk to Naldehra is along the highway.

Naldehra

As the nineteenth century came to an end, Lord Curzon, perhaps the most controversial viceroy that the colonising British ever sent to rule India, fell in love with the Naldehra. He would abandon the resplendent Viceregal Lodge in town and camp in the cedar woods of Naldehra for weeks on end – communicating with his office and sending messages that controlled one-fifth of the human race by heliograph. He was so enchanted by the

A SUBURBAN WALK

spot, that he even gave his youngest daughter Alexandra, 'Naldera' as her middle name after the place.

As a significant part of this romance, which was perhaps the most enduring one, he suggested the layout of a golf course on the site. This is a par 68 course with nine holes. It also has considerable character with wide views, a surround of woods and is completed by an ancient temple built in the local style right on the fairway.

Naldehra has a restaurant run by Himachal Tourism and a little ahead is the one in Chalets Naldehra. From Naldehra, you may walk back to town along the highway (or backtrack), hire a taxi near the golf course, or take a bus. If you have arranged it beforehand, a taxi from Shimla can meet you here.

A walk down to Sipur

If you are a good walker, take this option to Sipur, which is around two kilometres from Mashobra. At the Mashobra Bazaar, take a plunge down and then a climb back through the picturesque Mashobra valley which is matched by the tall Shali peak. The route holds thick woods where practically every tree of the region grows: Himalayan cedar, spruce, oak, rhododendron, horse-chestnut, birch and pine. Depending on the time of year, a variety of wildflowers drape the hillsides: the rhododendrons flower a dark red in spring, summer has banks of roses, daises and buttercups, and the monsoons speckle the luxuriant grass with lilies-of-the-valley and peonies. And through the year, flitting butterflies stab quick flashes of colour.

The path to Sipur takes a steady dip down the valley. The route is the track that adjoins the new Gables Hotel (the old one comprised the colonial structures that face the Mashobra Bazaar and belonged to the remarkable hotelier, Mrs F.E. Hotz.) Take this well marked route that skirts the building of the Mashobra School and has a sharp descent.

Past fields and orchards, and wood-and-slate houses you arrive at the glade of Sipur. The vicereine Lady Lytton once called it a 'tea-cup shaped valley' and it was popular for midnight picnics in the days of the Raj. Seven slim streams fed by freshwater springs nurture the soft grass of Sipur. The glade is held sacred to the local deity, Seep who 'visits' the spot at select times of the year. Shaded by colossal cedars, a little temple built in the local style with stone and wood, rests on an edge. An interesting element of folk carving exists on the eaves board of this temple which is over a century old. One panel shows what seem to be colonial Europeans – by their dress – shooting a tiger. The trees of Sipur 'belong' to the deity and villagers even dust their clothes and hair lest even a fine, needle-like leaf from a cedar be inadvertently carried away from the site.

127

Smaller shrines, merging with the woods are also there. This is the site of an annual Sipi fair held over the second weekend of May, and is a time for local matchmaking. The Sipi fair was also held regularly during the time when Shimla's European residents rubbed shoulders with the area's rural people. Today, at the fair there are stalls by the dozen and interestingly, many are run by Sikhs from the Hoshiarpur area; they travel from fair to fair in these hills and claim that their ancestors have been doing this for centuries.

From Sipur, you can walk back to Mashobra along the route you took on the descent, which will now be a steep climb. Excluding time spent at the glade, plan for at least two hours from Mashobra Bazaar.

Tips for Visitors

Getting there

By Rail: Kalka railway station is 90 kilometres from Shimla, and the one at Chandigarh is at a distance of 125 kilometres.

From Kalka, Shimla is connected by the narrow gauge Kalka-Shimla railway line.

By Road: Chandigarh is at a distance of 125 kilometres and Delhi is 375 kilometres away.

By Air: Chandigarh airport is at a distance of 130 kilometres, the one at Delhi is 395 kilometres away and Shimla airport at Jubbarhatti is at a distance of 22 kilometres.

Travel Combinations:

a. Travel by air to Delhi and then by rail or road.

b. Travel by air to Chandigarh, and then by road. Or fly to Shimla from there.

c. Travel by broad-gauge railway to Chandigarh or Delhi and then by road. Or take the narrow-gauge railway line directly to Shimla.

d. Taxis and buses are available for Shimla at all these places.

Come Rain, Snow or Sunshine

Practically all these walks can be undertaken at any time of year barring say a day of heavy rain or snow.

The monsoon normally breaks over Shimla in late June or early July and the weeks of steady downpour last till mid-

September. Apart from what may be a few hours of intense rain, the weather will not really come in the way of your holiday plans. Besides, the charm of the mist rolling in the valleys and entangling itself in trees, the presence of lush vegetation like the tree ferns, and magnificent sunsets (especially towards the end of the rains), will add to the experience of an enriching walk. Similarly, a day of snow may lead to a walk-disruption, but again, there is the rare pleasure of walking through a few inches of fresh snow. Winter temperatures may hover for a few days around freezing point, but otherwise they remain above this. Changes in the micro-climate and global warming have done their share by making the days of heavy snow (like six and a half feet standing in 1945) part of local history.

For the longer walks, a morning start is recommended; otherwise, just about any time of day is fine provided you wrap up by dark.

Equipment

For the walks, a comfortable pair of shoes is all you really need. For the hikes something preferably something with a good grip at the ankles, comfortable trousers, warm clothing appropriate for the time of year, personal gear like sunglasses, caps and cameras and prescription medicines may be added. Food and refreshments, sunscreen lotion and mosquito repellent, binoculars, walking sticks, first aid kit may also be added depending on your requirements. During the rains or in snow, appropriate footwear, a raincoat/jacket and an umbrella should be added.

The virtues of a walking stick

A walking stick comes in handy for most of these walks. It's a good support up the slopes and acts as a deterrent for wayward monkeys. These are available all over town at various souvenir shops, and the Lakkar Bazaar, just off the Ridge has several shops selling them at reasonable prices.

Precautions and suggestions

Persons suffering from heart conditions, epilepsy, lung disorders and asthma are advised not to take the strenuous walks. Also do not forget that you are 2,000 metres above sea level and require a little extra effort to breathe in any case.

Carry some water and a little snack. A folding or regular umbrella or a raincoat should also be carried, especially during the monsoons. Also be prepared for a drop in temperature after sundown, and wear or carry suitable clothes.

On the nature rambles do not leave the trail or spur, unless you are very sure of where you are going – distances and directions can be deceptive. While crossing a stream, do not step on a wet or moss covered rock. It can be very slippery. The Shimla hills do not have poisonous snakes except the banded krait and these are rarely, if ever, encountered.

You may encounter monkeys in certain areas like Jakho. They rarely attack unless threatened, or if foodstuffs are visible. Do not tease them, or look them in the eye or panic.

Some walks, especially in the suburbs, can be undertaken with connections made by bus or car, which are followed by the walk.

Barring a few 'dark spots', cell phones work in all the areas covered in the book.

You will be pleasantly surprised to find how helpful the local people are. Do not hesitate in asking for directions or assistance.

Please do not litter, especially with any non-biodegradable material like plastic bags, foil and cans.

Some local pronunciations

There are many colonial names that are still in use in Shimla. Going strictly by their 'correct' enunciation may leave you asking for directions to a place everyone knows about, but is clueless about where you want to go.

Boileauganj – Baloo Ganj

Sanjauli – Sunjoli or Sunjaoli

Annandale – Annadale

Bemloe – Bem-loee

Photo Credits

M.M. Singh

In text, by page number

II: Shimla view from Chotta Shimla

42: Auckland House

43: View of Tara Hall in winter

48: Observatory House

74: Raj Bhavan

115: View of Shimla's southern slopes

In colour photo pages (in order of succession)

In winter, a stretch down to the Mall from the Ridge

The Ridge after a light snowfall

A Swiss Bavarian style window at the Cooper Block of the Cecil

One of Chapslee's bedrooms

Viceregal Lodge, now the Indian Institute of Advanced Study

Blooms outside Viceregal Lodge

Khaleej Pheasant

Monal Pheasant

Manorville House

Christ Church at night

Ponies near Mashobra

Snow walk in Naldehra

The cedar forest of Shimla's water catchment area, near Charabra

Rest of the photographs are provided by the author.

Index

Kamru Nag Dhar, 93
Kamru Nag, 93, 94
Kangra, 8, 93
Kanlog, 101
Kapurthala, 55, 97, 108
Kariali, 95
Karna, 94
Kasauli, 10, 68
Kelston, 109, 110
Kendalls, 68
Kennedy Cottage, 16
Kennedy House, XI, 16
Kennedy, Charles Pratt, XI
Keonthal, XI, 10
Ker, Sir Arthur Milford, 108
Keylong, 94
Khadi Gram Udyog, 68
Khalini, 100, 103
Kiar Koti, 111
Kim, 19, 20, 115
King Henry XIII, 90
Kingsley Estate, 85
Kinnaur, 95, 124
Kipling, Alice, 19
Kipling, Lockwood, 19
Kipling, Rudyard, 12, 18, 19, 42, 68,
    69, 74, 80, 96, 109, 115, 123
Kipling, Trix, 19
Kitchener, Lord, 83
Klare, 100, 102, 103
Knockdrin, 2, 16, 34, 35, 39
Kolkata, XI
Koti Resort, 125
Kotshera House, 35
krait, 131
Krishna, Bhagwan, 117
Kufri, 95, 119
Kullu, 94, 124
Kumar House, 35, 39

L
'Longshanks' I, Edward, 76
Ladies' Mile, 85, 86
Lahaul, 94
Lahore, XI, 19, 66
Lakkar Bazaar, 18, 77, 82, 83, 89, 95,
    107, 111, 131
Lakshman (Laxman), 83

Lanka, 83
lath and plaster, 8, 12, 16, 121
Laureate Public School, 111
Law, Sir Edward, 20
Lawrence, John, XI, 10
Lawrence, Sir Henry, 10
Legislative Assembly Chamber of
India, 15-16
Legislative Assembly, 15, 16
Lhasa, 40
library, 71
Library, 78, 79
lichen, XIII, 6
Lieutenant Governor of the Punjab,
    85-86
Lloyds Bank, 31
Lloyd-Wright, Frank, 13
Lodge, the, 24, 25, 26, 59, see also,
    Viceregal Lodge
Lokayukta, 76
London, 4, 68, 70
Longwood Hotel, 109
Longwood spur, 108
Longwood, XV, 106, 107, 108, 109
Lord of Annandale, 76
Loreto Order, 12
Lovers' Lane, 64, 75, 86
Lower Bazaar, 68, 113, 114, 115, 118
Lower Himalaya, 94
Lower Kaithu, 39, 41
Lurgan Sahib, 20
Lutyens, Sir Edwin, 28
Lytton, Lady, 127
Lytton, Lord, 24, 123

M
Mackenzie, Colonel, XIV
Mahabharata, 94
Maharaja of Bharatpur, 110
Maharaja of Darbanga, 12
Maharaja of Dumraon, 12
Maharaja of Faridkot, 123
Maharaja of Patiala, 3, 73
Mahasu peak, 95
Mahasu, 95, 121
Mahun Nag, 94

Shimla

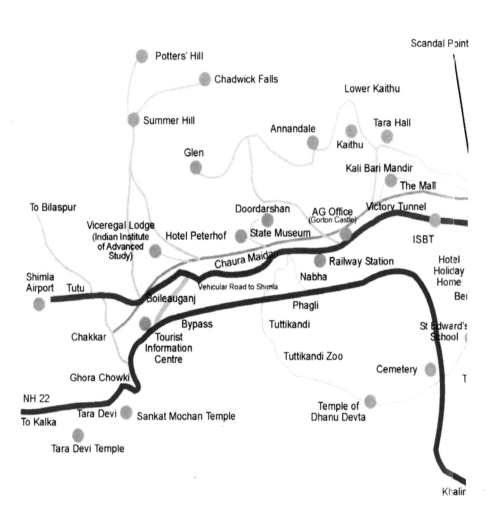

Potters' Hill

Chadwick Falls

Lower Kaithu

Summer Hill

Tara Hall

Annandale

Kaithu

Glen

Kali Bari Mandir

The Mall

To Bilaspur

Doordarshan

AG Office
(Gorton Castle)

Victory Tunnel

Viceregal Lodge
(Indian Institute
of Advanced
Study)

Hotel Peterhof

State Museum

ISBT

Chaura Maidan

Railway Station

Hotel
Holiday
Home

Shimla
Airport

Tutu

Vehicular Road to Shimla

Nabha

Boileauganj

Phagli

Bei

Chakkar

Bypass

Tuttikandi

St Edward's
School

Tourist
Information
Centre

Tuttikandi Zoo

Ghora Chowki

Cemetery

T

NH 22

Temple of
Dhanu Devta

To Kalka

Tara Devi

Sankat Mochan Temple

Tara Devi Temple

Scandal Point

Khalir

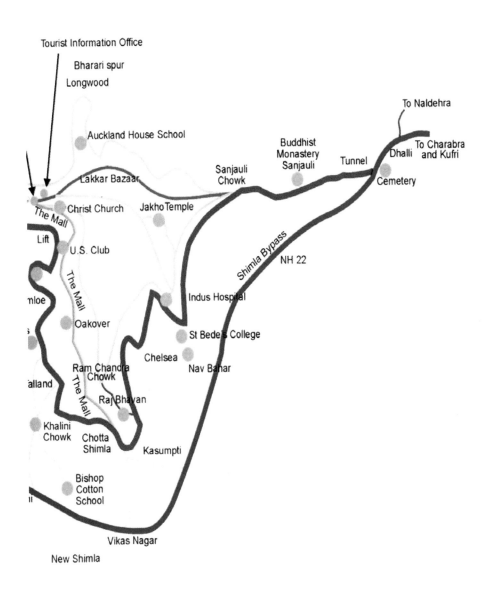

Tourist Information Office

Bharari spur

Longwood

Auckland House School

To Naldehra

Buddhist
Monastery
Sanjauli

Tunnel

To Charabra
and Kufri

Dhalli

Sanjauli
Chowk

Lakkar Bazaar

Cemetery

The Mall

Christ Church

Jakho Temple

Lift

Shimla Bypass

NH 22

U.S. Club

The Mall

Indus Hospital

mloe

Oakover

St Bede's College

Chelsea

Nav Bahar

Ram Chandra
Chowk

The Mall

Raj Bhavan

alland

Khalini
Chowk

Chotta
Shimla

Kasumpti

Bishop
Cotton
School

Vikas Nagar

New Shimla

19610495R00118

Printed in Poland
by Amazon Fulfillment
Poland Sp. z o.o., Wrocław